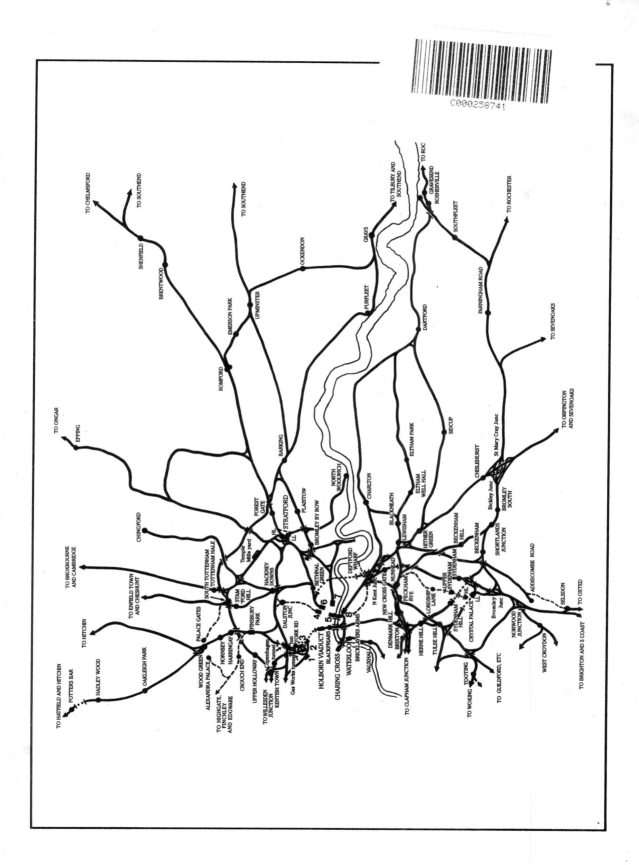

BRITISH RAILWAYS

PAST and PRESENT

LONDON

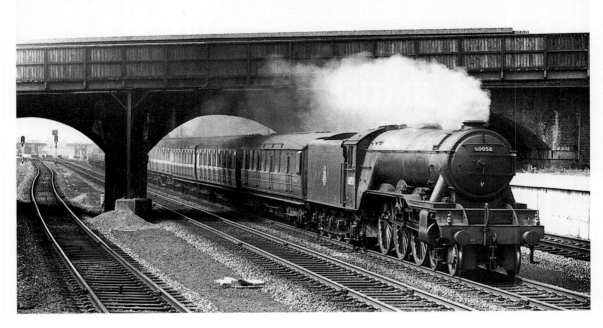

POTTERS BAR: The A111 road bridge south of Potters Bar station needed to be completely replaced as a result of the East Coast Main Line electrification programme. Steaming under the old spans on 16 July 1955, Gresley Class 'A3' 'Pacific' No 60058 *Blair Atholl* hauls an express for King's Cross. On 22 December 1987, Class '47/0' No 47288 brings a haul of southbound 'cartics' beneath the present-day structure. *Both Brian Morrison*

BRITISH RAILWAYS

PAST and PRESENT
LONDON

Brian Morrison & Ken Brunt

Silver Link Publishing Ltd

Originally published as 'British Railways Past and Present' No 7 North East, East and South East London (February 1991), and No 13 North West, West and South West London (July 1992)
First published in this combined volume October 1992

Maps drawn by Christina Siviter

Printed in Great Britain by Woolnough Bookbinding Ltd, Irthlingborough, and bound by The Bath Press, Bath

British Library Cataloguing in Publication Data

British Railways Past and Present. -
London. - New ed
 I. Morrison, Brian II. Brunt, Ken
 385.09421

ISBN 0 947971 99 8

Silver Link Publishing Ltd
Unit 5
Home Farm Close
Church Street
Wadenhoe
Peterborough PE8 5TE
Tel/fax: (08015) 4-4-0

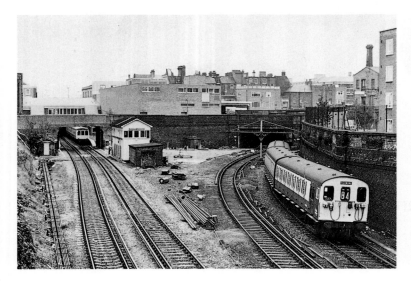

WESTERN JUNCTION, DALSTON: On 15 October 1984, the 10.37 Broad Street-Richmond train is formed of a Class '501' electric multiple unit (EMU) No 501157, while a Gloucester RC&W Class '119' cross-country diesel multiple unit (DMU) in the platform at Dalston Kingsland station awaits its passing before proceeding to Old Oak Common as empty coaching stock (ECS) following works attention at Stratford.

By 30 April 1991 the line from Broad Street has disappeared and the North London Line is electrified and runs through from North Woolwich to Richmond without the change previously necessary at Gospel Oak. Restarting from the Dalston Kingsland stop, Class '313' EMU No 313010 forms the 11.35 train from North Woolwich to Richmond. Very little has happened to the background buildings, and Western Junction signal box structure still exists together with Dalston Kingsland station, just visible beneath the road bridge. *Both Brian Morrison*

CONTENTS

NORTH ACTON: Apart from the station canopy having been lengthened, North Acton station remains relatively unaltered - even the fire buckets are still evident - from when it was photographed on 24 June 1956 as '5700' Class 0-6-0PT No 7791 scuttles towards Old Oak Common depot with a short van train. The lines on the far right from Paddington to High Wycombe, via Acton Wells, no longer see expresses to Birkenhead, but are still used for freight and the occasional special working or main-line diversion. The freight line into Old Oak Common, in the centre of the picture, has, however, long since vanished, although since the 'present' scene was recorded on 4 February 1990, one track has been reclaimed by London Underground in connection with its Central Line modernisation programme. *Brian Morrison/Ken Brunt*

INTRODUCTION

To compile a book of photographs depicting British Railways past and present, and give the capital city and its environs as reasonable a coverage as possible, it is first necessary to search out many old photographs, and then begin the not undaunting task of trying to duplicate the positions from which they were taken. Many of the 'past' photographs herein are from the 1950s, and are from my own collection. Of the remainder I am indebted to a number of colleagues and associates who have provided prints of locations which were not otherwise available, and in particular to a friend of many years standing, R. C. Riley, who has allowed me the pick of his extensive collection; as in the well-known lager advertisement, Dick really did find parts that others failed to reach!

In steam days lineside photographic permits were not difficult to obtain, and these allowed vantage points from signal gantries and signal boxes which, today, no longer exist. Therefore trying to stand in exactly the same place as the cameraman himself did many years before can sometimes be difficult, and it is for this reason that the desired elevation could not be achieved for a few of the present-day views. Similarly, lineside embankments were kept well cut back in steam days but, with the advent of modern diesel and electric traction, the risk of fire from hot cinders has been eliminated. In just one or two instances the spread of nature has made an exact copy impossible, although my co-author's adept wielding of a machete has opened up a number of old vistas and, in some cases, has saved British Rail expenditure for minor lineside deforestation!

As Great Britain's capital city, London boasts the most extensive railway network in the country. Prior to the abandonment of the railway regions (which in turn were based on the old railway companies), the Eastern, London Midland, Southern and Western Regions all had London termini, giving the city a remarkable total of 15 such stations. Holborn Viaduct and Broad Street have gone, but the others thrive, and most are either undergoing a major refurbishment or have recently had one completed.

The changes that have occurred to them over the past three or so decades have, in a few instances, been minimal: apart from the unwelcome addition (photographically speaking) of overhead electrification trappings, the King's Cross and St Pancras train sheds, for example, remain substantially unaltered, whereas Liverpool Street has been almost entirely rebuilt as part of the massive Broadgate development. The 'Windsor lines' side of Waterloo has taken shape as Waterloo International station for Channel Tunnel services, and Charing Cross, Cannon Street, Fenchurch Street and the Central Section side of Victoria all sport large developments above them. Marylebone has been extensively modernised and now utilises only two of the original three roof sections, and apart from modernisation of the concourse and renovation of Brunel's magnificent roof, Paddington has the unsightly signs of overhead electrification still to arrive. Euston was totally rebuilt in the less-enlightened 1960s.

Of the lines radiating out from these stations, differences between past and present are equally diverse, and branch lines such as Alexandra Palace, Brentford, Crystal Palace

High Level, Gravesend West, Merton Abbey, Palace Gates, Staines West and Uxbridge Vine Street have vanished altogether. Suburban services that once worked from Holborn Viaduct and St Pancras are now, for the most part, merged into the through 'Thameslink' trains, a part of the new Docklands Light Railway operates over the old Poplar branch, and track rationalisation/improvements abound almost everywhere.

The fate of London's famous steam locomotive sheds is variable in the extreme. On the positive side, Old Oak Common is still a major depot for diesel traction of all types, albeit with an uncertain long-term future, and Willesden houses and maintains the majority of electric motive power for West Coast Main Line services. Stewarts Lane looks after Intercity's 'Gatwick Express' locomotives and stock, in addition to diesel locomotives for both Network SouthEast Sector's Civil Engineers and Railfreight Sector, and stables large numbers of Southern EMUs. Stratford Works has closed down, but the maintenance depot survives for servicing diesel locomotives, Hornsey houses and maintains the 'Great Northern Line' EMU fleets, and Hither Green still plays an important role as a stabling and fuelling depot for a variety of Freight Sector and Departmental diesel locomotives.

Bricklayers Arms, Cricklewood, Camden, Devons Road, Kentish Town, King's Cross, New Cross Gate, Nine Elms, Norwood Junction and Plaistow have gone, together with the outlying depots of Epping, Feltham, Neasden and Slough; Southall remains as a haven for preserved steam, but with a much reduced capacity. The old sheds at Ilford and Strawberry Hill, however, have been given modern importance, and Wimbledon continues to care for the suburban electric units which ply their trade on 'South Western Line' services to and from Waterloo. Finsbury Park depot was built for the diesel era but is now derelict, having become one of the victims of the success of modern motive power technology where neither diesel nor electric-powered traction requires the extent of attention that once was the case.

Apart from the photographers already mentioned, thanks are in order to a number of British Rail personnel who were kind enough to provide facilities to duplicate some of the photographs which had to be taken from within their boundary fences, and to Derek Mercer, who undertook most of the printing from both old and new negatives, his expertise remaining undiminished - and a final word to the manufacturers of steel ladders, heavy-duty denim trousers, sturdy boots, sticking plasters and insect bite ointment, without whose products the preparation of this book would have been much less enjoyable than was the case!

Brian Morrison

Paddington

PADDINGTON (1): Despite the main concourse (or 'the Lawn' as it is known) being deepened to accommodate modern arrival and departure indicator displays, with a corresponding reduction in platform lengths, and despite the extensive renovations being carried out on the station, particularly to the roof, Brunel's great Paddington train shed has changed hardly at all since it was completed in 1854, except for additions and a few alterations brought about by traffic volume. At platforms 9 and 10 on 24 March 1951, 'Castle' Class 4-6-0 No 4096 *Highclere Castle* has brought in empty coaching stock to form an express for Bristol Temple Meads, while 'King' 4-6-0 No 6005 *King George II* approaches the buffer-stops with the 07.30 train from Shrewsbury.

At the same spot on 13 April 1992, Class '47/4' No 47636 *Sir John de Graeme* and Class '43' 'Intercity 125' power car No 43169 *The National Trust* make an extreme motive power contrast with, respectively, morning arrivals from Oxford and Bristol Temple Meads. The style of taxi has also changed somewhat! *Both BM*

PADDINGTON (2): Looking towards the buffer-stops from the country end of Paddington station, nothing of note has altered over the years apart from the motive power and coaching stock, and a change from bullhead rail to the modern flat-bottom variety - and there is a lot more rubbish in evidence! Shortly before withdrawal in 1953, the last Churchward 'Saint' Class 4-6-0 No 2920 *Saint David* waits to leave platform 4 with a special working for Swindon, the first coach of which was part of the GWR 'Centenary' stock introduced in 1935 for the 'Cornish Riviera Limited' and 'Bristolian' expresses.

At the same position on 14 May 1990, the 19.35 High Speed Train (HST) service for Penzance prepares to depart with Class '43' 'Intercity 125' power car No 43023 *County of Cornwall* providing appropriate front end traction.
Stanley Creer/KB

PADDINGTON (3): 'Castle' Class 4-6-0 No 5042 *Winchester Castle* approaches Paddington hauling an express from Cheltenham Spa on 1 June 1951, and passes the goods depot constructed on the site of the very first Paddington station.

Some 40 years later, the 14.15 local service from Reading is seen at the same position and is formed of Network SouthEast Sector-liveried Class '117' three-car DMU No L429. The lower portion of the goods depot brick wall remains but the 'Virol' sign has gone! The backdrop to the scene is now the elevated Westway approach to the M40 motorway. *Both BM*

RANELAGH BRIDGE: Apart from an occasional change of paint colour, the series of massive iron girder road bridges which span the lines into Paddington have not been altered since their construction. The same cannot be said for the track layout, however, which has been drastically 'rationalised'. On 3 August 1958 the 11.55 train for Pembroke Dock passes beneath Ranelagh Bridge in the charge of 'Hall' Class 4-6-0 No 4991 *Cobham Hall*.

As can be observed from the building to the rear of Ranelagh Bridge, this September 1989 scene was photographed from exactly the same standpoint, but the track on which *Cobham Hall* was travelling has been lifted. However, the lineside cabin is still intact, as the 16.10 service for Oxford commences its journey from Paddington powered by 'Class 47/7' No 47714 in Network SouthEast (NSE) livery with matching stock. *Both BM*

RANELAGH BRIDGE DEPOT: To avoid the necessity of constant trips back and forth to Old Oak Common Motive Power Depot (MPD) for fuelling purposes, locomotives which arrived at Paddington were able to re-fuel at nearby Ranelagh Bridge depot, a short distance down the line. The advent of HST services, however, removed nearly all locomotive haulage from Intercity working diagrams, and the fuelling point was no longer considered necessary. With classes '47', '50' and '52' prevalent, the fuelling point on 21 May 1975 was a busy place.

By September 1989, however, the whole area was derelict, and since this photograph was taken has been made into a car park. *Both BM*

WEST LONDON SIDINGS: Situated between Ladbroke Grove and Old Oak Common, West London Sidings were once a hive of activity with continuous shunting in progress to form goods and van trains of varying types. 'Castle' Class No 5094 *Tretower Castle* passes on 19 October 1957, hauling the 14.15 train for Worcester.

An 'Intercity 125' unit, with Class '43' power car No 43182 leading, forms the 10.25 Paddington-Paignton HST on 25 February 1990. Apart from the white building above the train, the scene today is barely recognisable. *R. C. Riley/BM*

Old Oak Common (81A)

OLD OAK COMMON YARDS: With a typical rake of suburban stock of the period in tow, '6100' Class Prairie tank No 6127 heads a Paddington-bound local service past Old Oak Common yards on 29 August 1959, and passes the new signal box under construction at the time (on the left) to replace the one opposite.

On 15 April 1989, the same scene shows the signal box (now nearly 30 years old), 'rationalisation' of permanent way, and empty space where the sidings used to be. A three-car Class '117' DMU No L412 forms the 11.30 stopping train from Maidenhead to Paddington, and Class '50' No 50037 *Illustrious* passes outbound with the 12.15 Paddington-Oxford 'Network Express'. Since this view was recorded, the tracks in the foreground which formed the spur up to North Pole Junction on the West London Line (see pages 34/5) have been removed to make way for the construction of North Pole International service depot to be used for Channel Tunnel stock. *R. C. Riley/BM*

OLD OAK COMMON SHED (I): Opened in 1906 and closed for steam traction in 1965, Old Oak Common Traction & Rolling Stock Maintenance Depot today is still a busy place, with two main sections, one for maintenance and repair of diesel locomotives and the other for maintenance of 'Intercity 125' units and DMUs. Outside the Repair Shop (which is still known locally as 'the Factory') on a miserable 21 November 1954, heavy repairs are under way on 'Castle' 4-6-0 No 5077 *Fairey Battle*, seen minus tender and a pair of driving wheels.

Outside 'the Factory' on Old Oak Common's Open Day of 17 August 1991 is paraded Class '50' No 50050 (restored to original livery with number D400), Class '47/4' No 47484 *Isambard Kingdom Brunel*, Class '31/5' No 31568 *The Enginemen's Fund*, and preserved Class '35' 'Hymek' No D7018. *Both BM*

OLD OAK COMMON SHED (2): No interior view of the shed at Old Oak could really convey its size. A lesser-known Churchward masterpiece, it comprised four 28-road roundhouses under one overall roof and was claimed by the Great Western Railway to be the largest of its type in the world. On 20 March 1955, fitted with condensing gear for working over the London Transport Metropolitan Line, Class '5700' 0-6-0 Pannier tank No 9706 rests inside one of the roundhouses.

Little remains of the 444 ft x 360 ft building today, and a car is parked where once the Pannier tank stood. The Class '08' shunter No 08454 rattling past would have been outside the original wall. *Both BM*

OLD OAK COMMON SHED (3): Seen alongside the shed office building on 5 May 1956, 'King' Class 4-6-0 No 6011 *King James I*, fitted with a double chimney, has the chalked legend on its smokebox door 'Brum O Man U 5'!

In somewhat altered form, and minus chimneys, the old building still exists today, but the adjoining blackened steam shed has been replaced by a three-road fuelling depot which, on 27 January 1990, contained a Class '08' shunter. *BM/KB*

Westward from Paddington

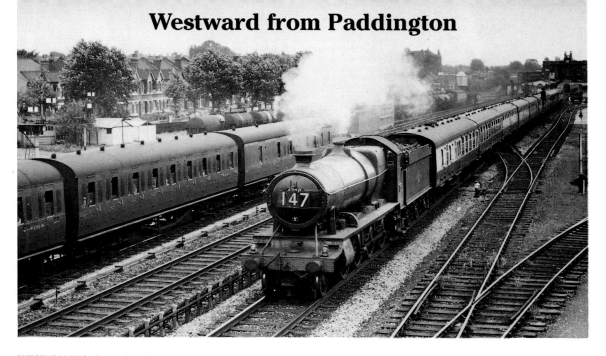

WEST EALING: Steaming freely through West Ealing on 10 August 1957, '4700' Class 2-8-0 No 4700 itself heads for the West Country with the 12.05 train from Paddington to Kingswear.

By 11 March 1992 the sidings have been sold off for business development, various buildings have sprung up in the background and the blackened station has received a welcome facelift. One of Intercity Sector's long-range-fuel-tank Class '47/4s', No 47826, scurries past with the 09.18 Brighton-Glasgow Central service, the 'Sussex Scot'. *R. C. Riley/BM*

SOUTHALL (I): Approaching Southall with a down goods train off the Brentford Dock branch on 10 August 1957, Class '5700' 0-6-0PT No 9641 passes its home shed of Southall; it carries the appropriate 81C shedplate on its smokebox door. Closed to passenger services in May 1942, the line remains open to the present day for freight only, but not as far as the old docks.

Coming off the branch with the 08.12 Sunday refuse train from Brentford Town Yard to Appleford waste processing plant on 11 February 1990 is Class '56' No 56038, rather inappropriately bearing *Western Mail* nameplates. *R. C. Riley/BM*

21

SOUTHALL (2): Hammering non-stop through Southall station on 5 May 1956, 'Castle' Class 4-6-0 No 5029 *Nunney Castle* (now preserved and restored for main-line running) heads for Paddington with an express from Bristol Temple Meads.

With the down-side platform buildings removed, and those on the up side having been rebuilt and shortened, a pair of NSE-liveried Class '50s', Nos 50023 *Howe* and 50035 *Ark Royal*, provide super-power for the 09.30 Oxford-Paddington train on 11 February 1990. *BM/KB*

SOUTHALL SHED (81C): The first engine shed at Southall opened in 1884. It was closed for steam in 1965, but remained open for the maintenance of diesel traction for a further three years, after which it stayed as a stabling point until 1986. Outside the eight-road shed on 11 June 1965 'Castle' Class 4-6-0 No 7029 *Clun Castle* is decorated with a GWR coat of arms ready to haul the 16.15 Paddington-Banbury train, the last regularly-scheduled steam working from the London terminus - 127 years after the broad-gauge *North Star* departed with the first passenger train.

Although the smoke outlet chimneys have been removed and the rails are becoming overgrown, the shed building remains intact, the premises now being used by the steam preservation movement as a London base for main-line steam. On 15 April 1989 Class '43' power car No 43191 *Seahawk* rushes past behind the fuelling bay, leading an 'Intercity 125' HST which is forming the 17.45 service from Paddington to Penzance. *Brian Beer/BM*

BRENTFORD DOCK: Under the auspices of the Great Western & Brentford Railway, the branch line from Southall to Brentford Dock had its beginnings in broad gauge days, opening for goods traffic on 18 July 1859, and for passengers on 1 May 1860. First leased to, and later vested in, the GWR, standard gauge was added in 1861, and by 1956 the combined merchandise and coal both forwarded and received totalled some 200,000 tons. '5700' Class 0-6-0PT No 8750 shunts the dock in March 1958.

The dock closed on the last day of 1964 and has since been developed as a marina, encircled by residential properties although, as mentioned on page 21, part of the branch remains open to serve Brentford Town Yard refuse transfer centre. However, passenger services, which were never of any particular significance, ceased in 1942, and it is reported that the last train was actually hauled by an unlikely class of locomotive, a 'Dean Goods' 0-6-0. *R. C. Riley/BM*

UXBRIDGE VINE STREET was the first GWR branch line in the London area and was solely broad gauge until 1871. It was also the first of the town's three stations, opening in 1856, and until 1904 enjoyed a monopoly of the town's rail transport. On 20 July 1952 the West Drayton & Yiewsley auto-train stands at the buffer-stops.

When the London Passenger Transport Board opened a new and spacious station in the High Street in 1938, the GWR's Vine Street station received a blow from which it never recovered; the final demise of passenger services came on 10 September 1962, with cessation of freight traffic on 13 July 1964. The site today is a car park for Post Office employees, with the modern building of Charter House in the background housing the head office of the Coca-Cola & Schweppes organisation. Although one platform face can still be discerned on the right, one could say that Vine Street station has been 'schwepped' away! *R. C. Riley/KB*

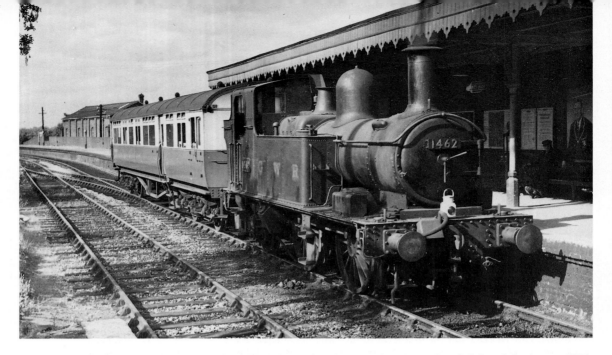

STAINES WEST: The single-line branch from West Drayton to Staines West opened to Colnbrook in August 1884, reaching Staines on 2 November of the following year. The line was a rural one, and passengers from the intermediate station of Yeoveney (initially Runnymede) were required to signal to the train driver to stop. Latterly a diesel railcar was used for passenger traffic, but when this photograph of the auto-train was taken on 20 July 1952 motive power was in the hands of '1400' Class 0-4-2T No 1462, which still shows the legend 'GWR' on the tanksides.

Passenger services to Staines West ceased in March 1965, but part of the line still remains open for freight traffic to Thorney Mill stone terminal, the remainder having been closed in 1991 when the Colnbrook oil terminal to the north of the station was no longer required. A line of tanks at the now closed oil terminal can just be discerned above the parked cars in the 1990 scene, with one track and both station wall and platform still in evidence. *R. C. Riley/BM*

IVER: On 27 May 1956, '6100' Class 2-6-2T No 6140 restarts a Paddington-bound local train from Iver.

Nearly 34 years on, the scene has hardly altered except for the elimination of the telegraph poles and the growth of a tree. Passing at speed through the station on 10 March 1990, Class '47/3' No 47315, in 'general-user' grey livery, powers the 10.00 Newbury-Paddington 'Network Express'. Calling at all stops, the steam-hauled services from Reading took a little under two hours for the journey to Paddington. Today a first-generation DMU is expected to cover the same schedule in around $1^1/_4$ hours. The advent of new Class '165/1' 'Thames Turbo' stock is scheduled to further reduce the journey to under the hour. *R. C. Riley/BM*

SLOUGH: A precursor of the 'Intercity 125' HSTs, one of the Metro-Cammell-built 'Blue Pullman' sets forms the 'Bristol Pullman' from Paddington on 10 October 1963, sweeping through Slough with semaphore signals indicating a clear road ahead.

Although a number of background buildings survive, indications of a diminishing railway dominance abound as the modern HST counterpart is seen at the same spot on 10 March 1990, forming the 12.00 Paddington-Swansea service. *R. C. Riley/KB*

West London Line

CHELSEA & FULHAM: The West London Extension Railway was opened on 1 April 1863, as a partnership between the LNWR, GWR, LSWR and LB&SCR, who, between them, formed the West London Joint Railways. The first station on the north bank of the River Thames was Chelsea & Fulham, which in company with the rest of the line lost its passenger services in the early days of the Second World War, on 20 October 1940. At the end of hostilities, the Joint Railways were unable to restore services as enemy bombing had badly damaged and even obliterated some stations and, in any event, the prospect of Nationalisation loomed and they were not prepared to spend money on repairs. On 6 February 1955, the station still stood but was demolished shortly afterwards.

Today the forecourt is a car park for a block of flats, and the railway is out of sight behind the brick wall. The background buildings on the left, however, appear unchanged. *R. C. Riley/BM*

CREMORNE VIADUCT: Dating from the opening of the West London Extension Railway in 1863, Cremorne Viaduct spans Chelsea Creek and takes its name from the once-famous pleasure gardens and pier which stood at the location. The viaduct was designed by the Chief Engineer to the LNWR, William Boker, and built in cast iron segments to compliment the style of other River Thames railway bridges. The trackbed was constructed to broad-gauge dimensions at the extra expense of the GWR, but little use was made of the third rail after the first few years. Popularly known today as Chelsea Bridge, the structure has six 120-foot-span arches over the water, and is 1,020 feet in length. On 27 December 1985, a Class '47' locomotive crosses the River Thames hauling the 09.58 Manchester Piccadilly-Brighton cross-country Intercity train.

Just over two years later, on 22 January 1988, Class '33/2' No 33204 is seen at the same place hauling a rake of EMU stock from Ilford Depot to Eastleigh Works for repair. In such a short period of time, what a difference to the surroundings! *Brian Beer/BM*

KENSINGTON OLYMPIA (1): At the end of the Second World War Kensington Addison Road station buildings were in a very poor state and were eventually dismantled in 1958. The south-west bay was rebuilt to accommodate London Transport's District Line trains and a new, small, station building was constructed on the site of the original down-side building and opened on 24 May 1966. At the same time a new 'Motorail' terminal shed was built on the site of the old north-west bay, but this was later abandoned and is now a car park. The station was renamed Kensington Olympia in 1946, when London Transport's special trains for Olympia exhibitions and the like commenced. On 20 August 1955 the 12.30 Hastings-Manchester train passes Kensington Middle box behind Class 'H2' 'Brighton Atlantic' No 32424 *Beachy Head*.

Kensington Olympia was given the status of an Intercity station when the Sector's 'Cross-London' services commenced in 1986, but these have not been the success anticipated and have since been severely reduced. The trains remaining still stop here, however, and the station is also still used by the peak-hour shuttle from Clapham Junction, popularly known as the 'Kenny Belle'. On 29 July 1989 a through passenger service again used the centre tracks when the 08.30 Victoria-Worcester 'Venice-Simplon Orient Express' (VSOE) special passed, hauled by Class '47/4' No 47828. Middle box and the majority of the semaphore signals have long since disappeared. *R. C. Riley/KB*

KENSINGTON OLYMPIA (2): Approaching the station and passing Kensington North Main box, 'Schools' Class 4-4-0 No 30915 *Brighton* hauls London Midland Region maroon stock forming the 11.05 Walsall-Hastings service on 22 August 1959.

Only Kensington South signal box remains at the present time, both North and Middle boxes having been demolished. Passing the same location on 7 June 1991 Class '60' No 60045 *Josephine Butler* works 'light engine' back to Stewarts Lane Depot. Just one re-positioned semaphore signal remains, the houses backing on to the line are now shielded by a little more foliage, and a roof extension has been built on to one of them. *R. C. Riley/Brian Beer*

NORTH POLE JUNCTION: Situated south of Mitre Bridge Junction (which provides the connection between the West London Line and the West Coast Main Line at Willesden), North Pole Junction connected the West London Line with the former GWR main line at Old Oak Common (see page 15). On 31 August 1957 another action study of the handsome 'Brighton Atlantic' No 32424 *Beachy Head* is provided, as it steams past the signal box hauling the 12.35 cross-country train from Leicester to Hastings.

At the same position on 15 April 1989 Class '47/4' No 47466 hauls train 1Z37, the 09.56 'Footex' special for Wanderers supporters from Wolverhampton to Aldershot for a cup game. Apart from a few lineside accoutrements which have appeared, plus the loss of the signal box name, the only other changes at this location at the time related to the track layout, which was simplified in 1969 by merging the down line to Old Oak Common with the up line for a short distance with a facing crossover; the track on the left, which went to the former GWR carriage depot, was lifted at the same time. In order to clear the way for Channel Tunnel carriage sidings, the junction has now been taken out of use, but the signal box remains to control Mitre Bridge Junction, whose own signal box has been demolished. *R. C. Riley/KB*

35

Waterloo

WATERLOO (1): The original 1848 Waterloo station was located where platforms 7 to 11 are today, and was a modest terminus for the LSWR, taking over from the original Nine Elms station which had opened ten years earlier. Like Topsy, the station grew and grew; today it is the biggest station on British Rail, covering over 24l acres, and was opened in its present form by Queen Mary in 1922. In 1953 problems were being experienced with the Southern Region's Bulleid 'Pacifics'; Gresley Class 'V2' 2-6-2s were borrowed from the Eastern Region for a short period and worked a number of services from Waterloo, including the prestigious 'Bournemouth Belle', here waiting to leave behind No 60896 on 20 May 1953.

Very extensive engineering works in connection with the Waterloo International terminal for Channel Tunnel trains commenced in 1990 and have resulted in the Windsor Lines platforms, which dated from 1860, being totally demolished. The new international station, however, requires much longer platforms than the edifice it is replacing and the total acreage of the complete station upon completion of the work will be even greater than before. Wessex expresses today are operated by the impressive-looking 'Class 442' 5WES EMUs. On 26 July 1990 No 2417 awaits departure time with the 10.32 train for Weymouth. A number of changes to the platform canopies are self evident, and the exterior of the station building itself is now considerably brighter following belated removal of post-war grime. *R. C. Riley/BM*

WATERLOO (2): All of London's termini were somewhat dark and forbidding for quite a long period after the Second World War, and indeed for a number of years following Nationalisation. Eventually boarded roofs were replaced with glass again, and what glass still remained was cleaned. Although the steam days scene was taken after dark, the difference between the two views taken of platform 11 and separated by more than 39 years is quite marked - and would not have been very different had they both been taken during daylight hours! On Leap Year Day 1952 'West Country' 'Pacific' No 34011 *Tavistock* awaits departure with an evening train for Basingstoke.

On 5 February 1992, two five-car Class 442 'Wessex Electrics', Nos 2412 and 2418, form the 10.32 for Weymouth and the 10.45 for Poole respectively. *Both BM*

WATERLOO (3): Trackwork into Waterloo station has been rationalised as far as possible during the years which have passed between the dates of these two views, but the approach roads inevitably remain complicated in view of the number of platforms which require to be served. On 28 June 1952 'Lord Nelson' Class 4-6-0 No 30865 *Sir John Hawkins* arrives with a summer extra from Bournemouth, as another Bournemouth train departs.

With the Red Lion pub building still remaining on the left, but with a block of flats now occupying the right background, 'Wessex Electric' No 2423 forms a train from Poole on 26 July 1990. *Both BM*

WATERLOO (4): Apart from the numbering, the 'Windsor Lines' platforms 16 to 21 gave arriving passengers the impression that this section of Waterloo was a station in its own right, as it was not possible to cross from platform 16 to platform 15 without first passing through the barrier and entering again on the other side of a wall. Also the spandrels of the cast iron columns supporting the glass roof were unlike anything in the main body of the station; in fact they dated from 1885, when what was first known as the 'North Station' was added. Probably due to its detachment from the rest of the station, the area of the 'Windsor Lines' platforms was chosen for the site of Waterloo International terminus for Channel Tunnel trains. Before total demolition commenced, all three types of Class '455' EMU were on view at the platforms on 20 June 1988, with Class '455/7' No 5722 forming the 12.43 for Windsor & Eton Riverside, Class '455/9' No 5906 working the 12.45 for Kingston, and Class '455/8' No 5873 having just arrived as the 11.23 from Woking via Hounslow.

At the same location on 3 May 1992 some semblance of order is beginning to return as the International station takes shape after two years of being nothing more than a very large hole containing a myriad of building works. *Both BM*

WATERLOO (5): Work on the LSWR's underground line from Waterloo to Bank station in the heart of the City of London, the Waterloo & City Railway, commenced in 1894, was completed in 1898, and was a very successful alternative to the fleet of two-horse buses which had previously carried commuters from Waterloo to Bank! Known to nearly everyone as 'the Drain', the Waterloo & City Railway runs beneath the River Thames on double track, and today the journey of 1 mile 1,012 yards is scheduled to take 6 minutes. One of the original Dick Kerr & Company single motor cars constructed in 1899 for off-peak services on the railway was photographed at Waterloo in November 1940.

The present-day view shows Class '487' stock built in the same year of 1940 by English Electric and now painted into NSE livery. As indicated by the advertisement on the tunnel wall, after a life of over 50 years this stock is now scheduled for replacement. The end of the lattice-work footbridge can just be glimpsed beyond the modern cladding in the top left-hand corner of the photograph. *C. J. Marsden Collection/BM*

41

WATERLOO (6): Forming the 13.58 service for Reading, Class '423' 4VEP No 7745 leads another unit of the same class away from the 'Windsor Lines' platforms on 11 June 1985.

With the modernistic structure of Waterloo International station taking shape in the background, Channel Tunnel trains will soon be using this part of the station, work having commenced in 1990 with the demolition of Waterloo signal box and the construction of a giant raft to widen the station 'throat'. The comparison between these two views makes it evident that the term 'past' is merely relative! *Both BM*

VAUXHALL: Originally known as Vauxhall Bridge, the station here opened on the same day as Waterloo, its four island platforms being built on a viaduct with stairway connections to the roads below. Until 1910 all trains for Waterloo were stopped here for tickets to be collected by a veritable army of railway staff, known to the passengers of the day as 'the Vauxhall Mob'! On 4 May 1957 'King Arthur' Class 4-6-0 No 30454 *Queen Guinevere* was photographed from the London end of the platforms heading a Waterloo-Basingstoke train.

On 31 May 1990 the track layout appears to have changed very little, but the background houses have vanished and the office blocks on the north side of the line have been extended. Class '455/9' EMU No 5901 brakes for the station stop, forming the 13.55 local service from Waterloo to Hampton Court. *Both BM*

Nine Elms (70A)

LOCO JUNCTION: On 6 September 1958 'Merchant Navy' 'Pacific' No 35021 *New Zealand Line* passes beneath Loco Junction signal box as it backs down to Waterloo to pick up stock. All locomotive movements between the main line and Nine Elms shed were controlled by this box, which spanned the tracks until the depot closed in 1967.

The view on 25 March 1990 had to be taken from over the barbed wire fencing erected around what is now the site of the New Covent Garden Market, and shows a Waterloo-Portsmouth Harbour EMU express working with 4BEP Class '412' No 2303 leading a 4CIG unit. Apart from the running tracks, nothing whatever appears to remain from the original scene, and Loco Junction is a junction no more. *R. C. Riley/KB*

STEWARTS LANE CHORD: Passing the site of the old Nine Elms complex on 7 June 1987, Class '73/1' electro-diesel No 73142 *Broadlands* powers the 10.34 (Sun) Weymouth-Waterloo service between Queenstown Road and Vauxhall stations.

Less than four years later the modernistic lighting standard to illuminate the Covent Garden Market car park remains to dominate the foreground, but the signal gantry has been moved and, in the background, construction of the new viaduct carrying the Stewarts Lane Chord is nearly complete. The chord links the classic Dover-Victoria route with South Western tracks, and will provide access for Channel Tunnel trains to Waterloo International station. Passing on 26 January 1992 is 'Pullman'-liveried Class '73/1' No 73101 *Brighton Evening Argus* hauling ECS from Clapham Yard to Waterloo. The locomotive was renamed *The Royal Alex'* at a ceremony at Brighton on 2 May 1992. *Both BM*

NINE ELMS SHED: After the closure of the original London & Southampton railway terminus of Nine Elms in 1848, three roads of the station were utilised as new running shed accommodation, a further six-road building being added a year later. These structures were replaced on the other side of the main line by a new seven-road through shed in 1865, and this in turn was superseded 11 years later by a spacious semi-roundhouse with access from two turntables. This sufficed for 20 years until a large 15-road straight shed was built alongside the roundhouse, forming the depot layout as it remained until closure in 1967. On 16 September 1968 Class 'H16' 'Pacific' tank No 30519 is seen on the depot in the position where the mobile hamburger and candy floss trader was to stand more than 20 years later providing fast food for customers to the New Covent Garden Sunday market. Currently nothing remains of the 70A shed site, it having been totally redeveloped as the new market complex. *Both BM*

South Western Lines

CLAPHAM JUNCTION (1): Situated at a point where the ex-LSWR lines from Waterloo meet the ex-LB&SCR lines from Victoria and the West London Joint Line to Kensington Olympia, Clapham Junction is proclaimed as 'Britain's Busiest Railway Station'. Actually situated some 1¼ miles from Clapham, the station was opened on 2 March 1863 in order to provide a convenient interchange between passengers of the three railway companies including those of the London Chatham & Dover Railway, which company had running powers from Factory Junction, on the Victoria-Herne Hill route, to Longhedge Junction. Rounding the curve through the station on the London-bound main line on 25 July 1956, BR Standard '5MT' 4-6-0 No 75075 hauls a Bournemouth West to Waterloo train, and passes Class 'E4' 0-6-2T No 32500 which is engaged in shunting stock in the adjacent yard.

Currently the scene is little changed, with modern-looking advertisement hoardings and lamp standards having replaced their 1950s counterparts, and the platform itself now looking rather the worse for the passage of many feet. Passing through is Class '421/5' 'Portsmouth Greyhound' 4CIG No 1305 leading the 13.06 'Network Express' from Portsmouth Harbour to Waterloo. *Both BM*

CLAPHAM JUNCTION (2): Clapham Junction's famous 'A' signal box was of LSWR design and dated from 1905. On 25 June 1951 'Merchant Navy' Pacific No 35005 *Canadian Pacific* propels the 15.54 Clapham Junction-Exmouth Junction empty milk tanks beneath the structure, prior to setting off via East Putney to the main line.

Stripped of its canopy and rebuilt, 'A' box was still in use on 31 May 1990 as Class '423/1' 4VEP No 3484 passed underneath forming the 14.50 train from Guildford to Waterloo.

The signalling centre at Wimbledon finally took over control of the main line out of Waterloo in April 1991, after which a gradual demolition of Clapham Junction 'A' box began. On 21 April 1992 just the gantry remains as Class '455/8' units Nos 5851 and 5830 pass, forming the eight-car 16.42 service from Windsor & Eton Riverside to Waterloo. *All BM*

50

CLAPHAM JUNCTION (3): Having traversed the West London Line, Stanier Class '8F' 2-8-0 No 48666 of Toton shed (18A) hauls a Willesden to Norwood freight up the sharp curve into platform 17 at Clapham Junction on 20 July 1951. Construction of a new power box is obscuring the view of LB&SCR-built Clapham 'B' box, while a concrete gantry has been erected in front of the semaphore signals to carry colour light 'starters' for the West London Line platforms.

On 2 June 1990 Class '47/4' No 47625 rolls into the same platform hauling the Saturday 07.25 'Intercity Holidaymaker' service from Manchester Piccadilly to Eastbourne. The 'new' power box is now itself out of use, while its predecessor 'B' box and its attendant signals are long gone. The colour lights are in place on their now blackened gantry, and the background buildings have changed out of all recognition. *BM/KB*

CLAPHAM CUTTING: Overtaking 4SUB electric units on suburban services from Victoria and Waterloo, Class 'S15' 4-6-0 No 30833 passes through Clapham cutting on 13 May 1963 with the 15.54 train from Waterloo to Basingstoke.
 Apart from the drains having been covered over and a new signal gantry being in evidence, little appears to have changed in the intervening years to 23 February 1992, as a specially-powered 'Solent & Wessex Wanderer' railtour passes the same spot hauled by Class '56' No 56020 and Class '33/1' No 33116, the latter providing train heating. *Stanley Creer/BM*

DURNSFORD ROAD: Dating from the advent of electrification in 1915, sheds and repair shops were built by the LSWR at Durnsford Road, Wimbledon, together with a generating station which supplied the system. Passing the Power House on 2 March 1957 rebuilt 'Merchant Navy' 'Pacific' No 35014 *Nederland Line* is in charge of the down 'Bournemouth Belle'.

Eventually the requirement of additional capacity for longer trains and improved services necessitated renewal and modernisation of the power supply system, and Durnsford Road Power House became redundant when all the current needed was taken from the National Grid; the quite handsome structure was finally demolished in 1965. On 25 March 1990 the 16.25 Waterloo-Portsmouth Harbour express service passes the site, formed of Class '412' 4BEP No 2306 leading Class '421/2' 4CIG No 1219. With Durnsford Road sheds replaced in 1974 by today's double-ended 'Wimbledon Train Care' depot, nothing remains of the original scene except for the little brick-built line-side hut, and even that has lost its door! *R. C. Riley/KB*

WIMBLEDON PARK CARRIAGE SHEDS: With 4COR 'Nelson' EMUs as the majority occupants of Wimbledon Park sheds on 2 March 1957, a London Transport District Line train of red-liveried 'R' Stock passes on the approaches to Wimbledon station.

Apart from the change in rolling-stock and the demise of the Durnsford Road Power House chimneys, the scene is much the same on 25 March 1990 as silver-liveried District Line 'C69' Stock passes stabled Class '455s' and a Class '423' 4VEP. Although having been turned around and also having its door removed, the small hut still manages to remain in situ, albeit tilting rather ominously. *R. C. Riley/BM*

WIMBLEDON (1): Passing Wimbledon 'B' box on 2 March 1957, the 13.30 Waterloo to Bournemouth and Weymouth express is powered by grubby 'Merchant Navy' 'Pacific' No 35027 *Port Line*. Travelling in the opposite direction, heading towards Wimbledon station, a local train is formed of one of the many four-car suburban units (4SUBs) which then existed, No 4514.

On 25 March 1990 a Waterloo-Weymouth semi-fast service passes the same location with Class '421/2' No 1243 leading. The track has been rationalised, the background buildings have been supplanted by 'modern' commercial structures, and the only remaining sign of the signal box is a section of protective railing. *R. C. Riley/KB*

WIMBLEDON (2): In steam days Wimbledon Yard was a thriving place where any number of locomotives could be seen at any one time engaged in a variety of activities. As late as the early 1970s rolling-stock was stabled there, a degree of shunting was still carried out, and the yard was the starting point for some freight traffic. Inhabitants on 2 March 1957 include Class 'C2X' 0-6-0 No 32553 and a pair of Class 'Q1' 0-6-0s, Nos 33017 and 33015.

By 23 June 1990 the BR Property Board had disposed of the site, which is now in private hands. *R. C. Riley/KB*

SURBITON station was opened by the London & Southampton Railway in 1838 and called Kingston, reflecting the railway's ambition to serve the town that successfully fought to keep it away - and has regretted it ever since! Before finally being accepted as Surbiton, the station carried the names Kingston Junction and then Surbiton & Kingston. It was resited seven years after opening, and completely rebuilt between 1936 and 1939. Here we have a second view of the 'South Western Suburban Railtour' of 2 December 1962 (see page 57) showing the Beattie 2-4-0WTs again (this time with No 30585 leading No 30587), departing from Surbiton and heading for Hampton Court Junction.

Today the once extensive goods yard and sidings are the official station car park, and a Sunday visit was necessary in order to avoid the comparison scene being almost totally obscured by cars. Taken from the same standpoint, Class '455/8' No 5857 moves away, forming a service for Hampton Court. *Stanley Creer/BM*

HAMPTON COURT BRANCH: The short branch line to Hampton Court station, situated on the south bank of the River Thames near Hampton Court Palace, first opened for horse traction in 1849, and was once proclaimed as 'the station for East and West Molesey'. Today the branch is operated almost exclusively by Class '455' units which ply their trade to and from London on a half-hourly basis, but there was a time when a steady diet of EMUs could be supplemented to some extent by the daily goods train, which used to be steam-hauled down the branch. On 16 December 1959 '700' Class 0-6-0 No 30699 was the engine in use.

Approaching its destination on 21 February 1992 is Class '455' No 5859 as the 10.55 from Waterloo, seen at the same position on the line but photographed nearer the tracks, the encroaching vegetation making a more accurate and wider view impossible. *Terry Gough/BM*

CHESSINGTON SOUTH: The last line to be constructed by the Southern Railway, the 4¼-mile branch to Chessington South was intended to provide a railway service to new housing estates springing up south of Surbiton, but by the time the construction reached its present position the Second World War was imminent and precluded any further progress. Thereafter the 'Green Belt' effectively halted further housing developments in the area south of Chessington, and the original intention of continuing the line to Leatherhead never materialised. On Derby Day, 2 June 1954, the Royal Train left from Chessington South instead of the more usual Tattenham Corner station. Awaiting arrival of the Royal party is a suitably groomed 'West Country' 'Pacific', No 34011 *Tavistock*.

With the brick-built platform building now razed, and the opposite platform out of use, the 12.16 service for Waterloo awaits the appropriate time for departure, formed of Class '455/7' EMU No 5705. *BM/KB*

EPSOM: The present Epsom station site dates from 1859, although the railway first reached the town in 1847 when the London & Croydon Railway's Epsom Town station was opened. Epsom townsfolk enjoyed two stations until 1929 when the 'Town' closed, remaining open for freight only until 1965. On 25 March 1979 the distinctive 1928-dated Southern Railway overhead wooden signal box spanning the tracks was still in use and controlling the departure of Class '415/1' 4EPB No 5105 in the platform, forming the 14.12 Waterloo-Effingham Junction service.

Today Epsom commuters are almost spoilt for choice with their variety of services, and are able to travel direct to a choice of four London termini - Blackfriars, London Bridge, Victoria and Waterloo - using NSE's 'Thameslink', 'South Western Lines' and 'South London Lines' trains. On 21 February 1992 little has changed visibly at the location, although the signal box has lost its name since being taken out of use on 29 July 1990, when control was transferred to a new signalling centre at Wimbledon. The Class '455/9' EMU No 5907 in the platform has just arrived as the 13.18 train from Waterloo. *Both BM*

KINGSTON: Although the inhabitants of Kingston, and especially those with coaching interests, fought to keep the railway away from their town, and thus lost the opportunity to possess a main-line station in favour of nearby Surbiton, their present-day descendants enjoy four trains an hour to and from Waterloo, two Shepperton line services and two Kingston Loop trains via Strawberry Hill. The present-day station dates from a major reconstruction in 1934-35, prior to which the site comprised two levels, through lines at high level, and a terminus, known as Kingston Town, at street level; only the high level station now remains. Shunting the quite large Kingston goods yard on 4 June 1962 is Bulleid 'Austerity' Class 'Q1' 0-6-0 No 33011.

BR closed the yard in 1966, but the quite elaborate goods shed still stands and, on 5 February 1992, was in use for storage purposes by a company of bulk carriers; their lorry trailers now occupy the muddy yard. *Terry Gough/BM*

PUTNEY: Served by Guildford and Windsor Line trains, in addition to those for the Kingston and Hounslow Loops, Putney is a busy station situated at the junction of Putney High Street and Richmond Road. Passing through the station on 15 August 1965 is the 'Western Ranger' railtour, organised by the Locomotive Club of Great Britain and powered by BR Standard Class '4MT' 4-6-0 No 75066.

With new buildings having replaced the rather ramshackle-looking ones on the south side of the line, and with a lot of the railway now shielded from view by trees, the 16.30 Waterloo-Reading service passes the same spot on 30 April 1990 formed of Class '423/1' 4VEP stock, Nos 3468 and 3428. *Stanley Creer/BM*

BARNES: The location of Barnes station dates from the opening of the line to Richmond in 1846, and it is presently well served by the majority of trains which call at Putney. The main station building is an elegant affair with tall chimneys and steep gables, but is partly obscured by the rather ugly platform canopy on the London-bound side. On 25 March 1962 a Waterloo-Kingston-Waterloo roundabout service restarts from the staggered platform formed of 4SUB EMU No 4385.

With one of the platform buildings demolished, and both Rocks Lane bridge and the station edifice nicely cleaned, present-day Class '455/8' EMU No 5865 forms the 16.05 Waterloo-Hounslow Loop service. *R. C. Riley/BM*

HOUNSLOW JUNCTION: The Hounslow Loop line was authorised to the Windsor, Staines & South Western Railway by an Act of 1847, with the provision of a service to Hounslow being one of its main objectives. The line runs from Barnes Junction to Hounslow Junction, and from there has connections to the Reading line via both Feltham and Whitton. On 30 April 1966 a special train organised by the RCTS returns from a visit to the Longmoor Military Railway and approaches Hounslow at Hounslow Junction, hauled by the last two Class 'U' 'Moguls' to be withdrawn from service, No 31791 piloting No 31639.

New houses and an abundance of foliage record the passage of time as Class '455/7' unit No 5701 passes the same location on 3 May 1990 forming the 14.20 train from Guildford to Waterloo. *Stanley Creer/BM*

Feltham (70B)

FELTHAM SHED (I): The final engine shed to be built by the LSWR, Feltham was completed in time for the Grouping of 1923, and was the first major depot in Great Britain to be constructed in concrete, setting a pattern upon which the Southern Railway would enlarge during the next 15 years. The six-road structure could hold 36 locomotives, which were essentially freight types used for hauling the variety of goods traffic generated from the large Feltham Hump Yards. The depot survived until the end of steam on the Southern Region, closing on 9 July 1967. The yards survived a few more years, but eventually succumbed to the run-down of wagonload freight. One of the many varieties of locomotive allocated to 70B was the '700' Class 0-6-0; No 30567 is depicted here outside the shed building on 21 May 1955.

An extensive area of wasteland now exists where once there was a hive of activity, and a wooden lighting post (the same one?) is the only remaining link between these two scenes. *BM/KB*

FELTHAM SHED (2): Running alongside the eastern end of Feltham shed was a single-ended repair bay, seen here with a Birmingham R&CW Type 3 diesel (later Class '33') and Classes 'Q1' and 'H16' steam locomotives outside. Amid the present-day wasteland scrub, just one wall of the building survives. *Lens of Sutton/KB*

North London Line

UPPER HOLLOWAY: Popularly known as the 'Tottenham and Hampstead' route, the present-day Gospel Oak to Barking line links the former Midland Railway and LNWR systems with those of the former Great Eastern and London, Tilbury & Southend companies. Over the years the line grew on a piecemeal basis, with the present-day western extremity to Gospel Oak opening in 1888 and being $12^1/4$ miles from the eastern end of the railway at Barking. In addition to quite frequent cross-country freight trains, the route carries a Monday to Saturday half-hourly DMU service, connecting with Richmond-North Woolwich trains at Gospel Oak, and with LT&SR and LUL District Line trains at Barking. Approaching the Upper Holloway stop on 15 October 1984, the 14.45 train from Gospel Oak to Barking is formed of a two-car Birmingham RC&W Class 104 DMU.

   On 30 April 1990 new industrial buildings have appeared alongside the line, and the Midland Railway signal box and its attendant semaphore signals have disappeared. In the siding is one of the few remaining Class '104' DMU units (now smartened up a little with NSE livery), and passing is a Pressed Steel Company Class '121' single car unit No 55030 forming the 12.45 Gospel Oak-Barking train. *Both BM*

GOSPEL OAK: As well as being the terminus for trains from Barking, Gospel Oak is an interchange for North Woolwich-Richmond services which operate every 20 minutes from Monday to Saturday, but strangely are not considered as being worth a Sunday service. In addition to these 'North London Lines' passenger trains, a considerable amount of freight traffic utilises the tracks through Gospel Oak Junction. Hauling a rake of empty HTV coal hoppers on 15 October 1984, Stratford-based Class '37s' Nos 37166 and 37044 head for home round the curve through the west end of the station.

A few months after the 'past' view was recorded the signal box was destroyed by fire, to be replaced in 1985 by the unlikely-looking wooden structure being passed on 4 April 1992 by Class '313' EMU No 313022 forming the 14.43 Richmond-North Woolwich train. Signalling is now of the multiple-aspect colour light variety, and the 'starter' is now situated behind the camera on the end of a now shortened platform. *Both BM*

HAMPSTEAD HEATH: At a time when trains from Richmond operated through Hampstead Heath and Gospel Oak to Broad Street terminus, Class '501' EMU No 501164 picks up speed again after the Hampstead Heath station stop on 15 October 1984, and heads for the now demolished City of London station (see page 262).

Following the demise of the Class '501' units, services on this line were in the hands of Southern Region Class '416/3' 2EPB EMUs for a period, but are now operated by the more modern Class '313' EMUs which were constructed in 1976-77. On 4 April 1992 No 313016 forms the 14.03 train from Richmond, which now travels the $22^1/_4$ miles to North Woolwich in 1 hour 6 minutes, including no fewer than 26 stops! The lineside allotments are still in evidence, a small brick retaining wall has been built on the left, and the small lineside electrical box has received some unwelcome graffiti. *Both BM*

KENSAL GREEN JUNCTION: Situated between Kensal Rise station and Willesden, the junction at Kensal Green carries a large amount of cross-country freight traffic, in addition to the regular Richmond-North Woolwich passenger services. On 20 May 1984 Class '50' No 50032 *Courageous* passes with a train consisting mainly of empty Mk III sleeping cars from the overnight train from Penzance to Paddington, *en route* to Willesden for servicing at Willesden Carriage Depot (later known as Wembley Intercity Depot). The train reversed here at Kensal Green then, with the Class '25' on the other end leading, took the tracks on the extreme right to its destination, the devious routing being caused by a Sunday engineering possession.

Kensal Green Junction was remodelled and re-signalled in April 1985, rendering the signal box and semaphore signals redundant. On 4 April 1992 Class '33/0' No 33026 *Seafire* runs through the junction 'light engine', returning from Willesden Yard to the Southern Region. Again, a reversal has to be made here in order to take the line to the left which will gain access to home territory via Kew East Junction. Only one of the three background cooling towers now remains. *Brian Beer/BM*

ACTON WELLS JUNCTION: The North & South Western Junction Railway (N&SWJR) line from Willesden to Kew dates from 1853, and the focal point of the 3³/₄-mile line is Acton Wells Junction where five routes converge. From the north, there is the ex-N&SWJR line itself, the Midland line from Brent, and the route from Willesden High Level. From the south, the N&SWJR line runs to Kew, and a spur runs down alongside the ex-GWR main line into Acton Yard. From Kew, trains can diverge again either via Barnes or Brentford. On 4 May 1957 a transfer freight for Southern Region metals at Feltham passes the junction, hauled by ex-LSWR Urie Class 'H16' 'Pacific' tank No 30516.

Although the semaphore signals have been deposed by multiple-aspect colour light signalling, the ex-North London Railway Acton Wells Junction signal box, *circa* 1892, still controls the junction as, on 4 April 1992, USA-constructed Class '59/1' No 59101, later named *Village of Whatley*, passes with empty ARC hoppers from Allington, Kent, heading for the GWR main line and back to Whatley Quarry, via Acton. *R. C. Riley/BM*

Marylebone

MARYLEBONE (1): The Victorian visionary Sir Edward Watkin brought his Manchester, Sheffield & Lincolnshire Railway into London by its own difficult route, partly sharing the Metropolitan Railway's main line. He called it the Great Central Railway, and the first train steamed into the new terminus of Marylebone in March 1899. The Great Central Railway was the last main line to be constructed into London, and it was the first to disappear when all through services beyond the Chiltern Hills ceased on 3 September 1966, leaving the station with no trains beyond Aylesbury or Banbury. BR's Eastern Region continued local services until, after a brief spell of Western Region control, the London Midland Region was given the job of running down and overseeing an eventual closure. It was planned for High Wycombe trains to be diverted into Paddington, and for Aylesbury line travellers to be accommodated by a shuttle to Amersham, and thence to Baker Street. However, the advent of BR's Network SouthEast Sector in 1986, and its first Managing Director, Chris Green, in particular, brought about an upturn in Marylebone's fortunes which, today, has been completely modernised, both with regard to the refurbished station and its new trains.

The first view (above left) shows the station in 1981, when the train shed had three roof sections.

The same view on 28 February 1991 (left), during the refurbishment programme, shows only two of the three roof sections now remaining, and a Class '115' DMU departing as the 12.10 train for Aylesbury via Amersham.

The modern station is seen above on 22 March 1992, with Class '165/1' 'Chiltern Turbos' Nos 165011/024 departing as the 13.27 to High Wycombe, and others of the same class stabled in the new sidings on the right. *All BM*

MARYLEBONE (2): There was a time when Marylebone boasted a titled train, 'The Master Cutler' to Sheffield. On 5 July 1952 Class 'A3' 'Pacific' No 60052 *Prince Palatine* carries the appropriate headboard as it winds the service out of the terminus. Milk tank wagons working from the Shrewsbury area can be seen in the milk depot to the left.

Today the near tracks are used only to gain access to the train washer, and only the two far lines are used for incoming and outgoing traffic. On 19 March 1992 the 14.44 departure for Aylesbury is formed of a mish-mash of Class '115' DMU stock, with Driving Motor Brake Standard (DMBS) No 51655 leading. The background buildings and the bridge remain, but the milk tanks and the signal gantry are but memories past. *Both BM*

MARYLEBONE (3): In early 1962 four BR Standard 'Britannia' 'Pacifics' were allocated to Neasden shed and oper-ated many of the main-line trains from Marylebone. Despite their somewhat run-down condition, three of them remained on the line until the depot closed, when they were transferred to Annesley. The class was then re-intro-duced to ex-GCR metals when eight were allocated to Banbury, and they saw out the last 12 months of Marylebone's main-line workings alongside the then new DMUs which were operating the suburban services. Retaining nameplates from happier days on the Scottish Region, No 70053 *Moray Firth* slugs up the 1 in 100 gradi-ent out of the station on 5 February 1964, and approaches Lord's Tunnel with the 14.38 train to Nottingham.

In the same position, but heading towards the terminus, Class '165/0' No 165027 forms the 13.30 from Banbury on 19 March 1992. The background building still stands and, surprisingly, so does the lighting pole. *P. J. Lynch/BM*

Neasden (34E)

NEASDEN SHED: Opened by the Great Central in 1899, Neasden shed serviced and maintained locomotives for both Marylebone main-line and suburban trains, and in addition provided necessary facilities for motive power working into and from Neasden Yard. Probably the most cosmopolitan of all steam depots, engines from five different BR Regions could often be seen under the one roof. After Nationalisation, the depot was given the code 34E by the Eastern Region, but became 14D for the last four years of London Midland Region control when arrival of diesel units for the Marylebone suburban services resulted in closure in 1962. At about that time, with both engine allocation and staff transferred to Cricklewood (14A), the depot stands deserted.

No trace of the depot or the marshalling yards remains on 21 March 1992. *Lens of Sutton/BM*

Chiltern Lines

NORTHOLT JUNCTION (1): Fierce competition with the LNWR for passenger traffic between London and Birmingham led to a GWR requirement to shorten its lengthy route through Oxford. At the same time the GCR wanted an alternative access to London, as the Metropolitan Railway's lines were congested and the company uncooperative. Their common cause resulted in a new line being built from Old Oak Common through the Chilterns to High Wycombe and beyond. It was owned by the GWR as far as Northolt Junction, but thereafter came under the auspices of a GW&GC Joint Committee, incorporated in 1899. Running on the down line beneath the GWR main line to gain the Joint metals on 4 May 1957, Class 'B1' 4-6-0 No 61028 *Unseke* heads for Manchester (London Road) with the 12.15 express from Marylebone.

On 24 February 1992 Class '165/0' 'Chiltern Turbo' No 165027 rounds the same curve forming the 12.40 service from Marylebone to Banbury. Trees have replaced the telegraph poles, and the encroaching foliage is looking rather menacing. *R. C. Riley/BM*

NORTHOLT JUNCTION (2): This quite remarkable and previously unpublished photograph shows 'King' Class 4-6-0 No 6020 *King Henry IV* hauling a relief to the 18.10 Paddington-Birkenhead express on 4 May 1957 passing Northolt Junction as the 18.20 Marylebone-Sheffield express passes beneath, hauled by Class 'A3' Pacific No 60107 *Royal Lancer*. It was certainly extremely lucky for the photographer that the two trains should pass this location at exactly the same time, but how many would have taken full advantage of the situation as Dick Riley has done here? The two trains did not, of course, collide at the converging junction ahead (where in any event there was quadruple track as far as West Ruislip), as the Sheffield one was travelling very slowly until it received a favourable signal!

Today exactly the same photographic vantage point is not available, but this view at the same location clearly shows the present state of the old GWR main line, where one of the two tracks is in process of being taken up, while the remaining one is rusted as a result of infrequent use; Birmingham traffic from Paddington has long since reverted to its circuitous route through Oxford. In the background a London Underground Central Line train of 1962 Stock passes, forming a service from Loughton to West Ruislip. *R. C. Riley/BM*

SOUTH RUISLIP: On FA Cup Final day, 1957, an up supporters' special working to Wembley is halted in South Ruislip station platform awaiting arrival of an Eastern Region guard for the run down the GC route into Wembley Hill station, while a Bicester-Paddington Army leave train passes on the through road. Both trains are worked by 'Hall' Class 4-6-0s, Nos 5927 *Guild Hall* and 6924 *Grantley Hall* respectively.

On 24 February 1992 the 12.30 Banbury-Marylebone service runs non-stop through the station formed of Class '165/0' No 165009, the '1' of the number having peeled off. The wooden platform shelter on the down side has been replaced with a glass box-like waiting room, the station building on the up side has been superseded by a like structure, and a new platform is evident, having been constructed over the old up slow line, leaving just the one through line instead of the original two. *R. C. Riley/BM*

DENHAM (I): Passing Denham West Junction signal box, and crossing the 181-yard viaduct over the Grand Union Canal to the south of Denham, '2251' Class 0-6-0 No 2290 hauls a goods train destined for Neasden Yard on 11 April 1953.

   On 24 February 1992 'Chiltern Turbo' No 165006 forms the 10.45 service from High Wycombe to Marylebone and crosses the viaduct at the same point. Concrete sleepers and continuous rail replace the old bullhead variety, and there is no longer any trace of the semaphore signals and attendant signal box. *Both BM*

HARROW-ON-THE-HILL: The original station here was opened in 1880 as part of the Metropolitan Railway's 'extension' to Chesham and Aylesbury. When running powers to South Harrow Junction were obtained by the GCR, the station became part of the Metropolitan & GC Joint Line, and from 1899 passengers were able to travel into London by 'Metropolitan' services to Baker Street or to Marylebone on the Great Central trains. With suburban facilities into London inextricably linked, the station was rebuilt and expanded between 1938 and 1948, and passengers still have a choice of travelling by BR or London Underground services. On 28 July 1981, the 14.40 Aylesbury-Marylebone train restarts from the Harrow-on-the-Hill stop, formed of a four-car Class '115' DMU in three different liveries!

The same scene in 1992; the town of Harrow continues to grow, and Class '165/1' No 165022, in the latest version of NSE livery, leaves as the 13.39 service from Aylesbury to Marylebone. *Both BM*

NORTHWOOD HILLS: On 16 May 1964 the four-coach 14.38 Marylebone-Nottingham Victoria train passes Northwood Hills hauled by BR Standard '5MT' Class 4-6-0 No 73011.
  There is always some trepidation when setting out to try and copy a picture from the past which includes a railway embankment in the foreground, as in so many cases the absence of attention to growth by both steam locomotive and BR employee over the years results in a reasonable duplicate of the scene being impossible. In most cases the location is discarded, and in the normal way this would have been the case here, but just one example of the problem was thought appropriate for this book! Behind the small woodland that has sprung up lineside at Northwood Hills, a Baker Street-Amersham Metropolitan Line train of LUL 'A' Stock passes the same location. *P. J. Lynch/BM*

Victoria

VICTORIA (1): The first Victoria station was opened by the LB&SCR in 1860, and allowed usage by the London Chatham & Dover Railway (LC&DR) until the latter's own adjoining terminus, shared with the GWR and its trains from Southall, was completed in 1862. Even after rebuilding was completed in 1909 the stations remained as separate entities, with their own individual entrances, platform numbers and station masters, and did not become one until 1924. The 'Chatham side' of Victoria consists of platforms 1 to 8, which, despite the extensive developments that have taken place above the 'air space' of the 'Central' portion of the station, remains relatively untouched by the passing years. On 4 April 1953 the 14.35 train for Ramsgate departs from platform 2, powered by 'Battle of Britain' 'Pacific' No 34072 *257 Squadron*, a locomotive which has been preserved and is still active today.

Showing headcode '14' for a Folkestone Harbour train travelling via Herne Hill and Bat & Ball, Class '411/5' 4CEP No 1550 awaits departure from the same platform on 7 April 1992. *R. C. Riley/BM*

VICTORIA (2): With only scars in the wall to show where Victoria (Eastern) signal box once stood, the same trains as shown on the previous page depart from Victoria on 4 April 1953 and 7 April 1992 respectively. The background buildings appear a mite cleaner, and two roof extensions have been built. Rather surprisingly, however, they appear otherwise to remain relatively untouched. *R. C. Riley/BM*

VICTORIA (3): Wearing the drab 'BR Corporate Blue' livery in which most locomotives were painted from the middle 1960s through the 1970s, Class '73/1' No 73140 departs from Victoria with the 'VSOE' bound for Folkestone Harbour.

With the eastern wall of the Victoria Place development above the 'Central' side of the station now providing the background, Class '411/5' 4CEP No 1513 departs from the same platform on 7 April 1992, forming the 10.23 service for Dover Priory. *Stanley Creer/BM*

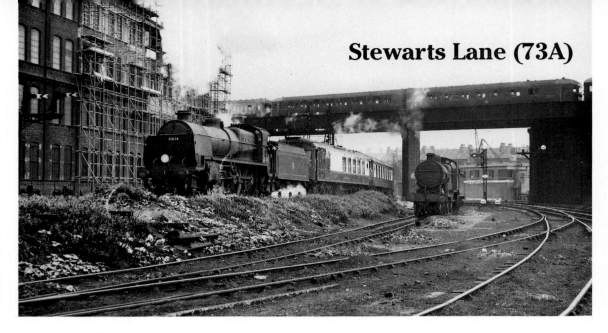

Stewarts Lane (73A)

STEWARTS LANE SHED (I): The LC&DR Works Depot at Longhedge was established in the early 1860s, and the locomotive shed was rebuilt in 1881 from a half roundhouse to a straight shed. After the LC&DR merged with the South Eastern Railway in 1889 the premises became too small for the facilities required and the workshops were transferred to Ashford, Kent. The former erecting shop was retained for engine repairs to be carried out, and the carriage works became the carriage shed. Following closure of the ex-LB&SCR shed at Battersea Park, the Southern Railway further improved the depot, which was renamed Stewarts Lane in 1934, after the station of the same name which had been opened nearby by the LC&DR in 1863, but closed again just four years later. With Class 'El' 4-4-0 No 31067 in the shed yard, the 'Golden Arrow' Pullman empty coaching stock from Victoria is brought into the depot for servicing on 18 August 1957 behind Class 'U' 'Mogul' No 31624. The stock is passing beneath the main line from Victoria, over which runs a six or eight-car rake of Class 2HAL EMU stock.

Nearly 30 years later the viewpoint has changed little, as a Class '411' 'Kent Coaster' EMU passes, forming a Victoria-Folkestone Harbour boat train. *R. C. Riley/BM*

STEWARTS LANE SHED (2): Prior to hauling out a rake of carriages for a late summer train from Victoria to Dover on 31 September 1957, Class 'U1' 'Mogul' No 31903 has its coupling checked.

At the present time Stewarts Lane Traction & Rolling Stock Maintenance Depot (as it is now titled) maintains 'Gatwick Express' locomotives and stock for the Intercity Sector, locomotives for Railfreight's Trainload Construction and for the NSE Civil Engineers, and also acts as a stabling point for a variety of South Eastern Section EMUs. Known today as the 'EMU shed', the same premises on 6 April 1992 are occupied by Class '415/4' and '415/7' 4EPBs Nos 5473 and 5627, the latter being one of six EMUs used with 'Kent Coast' express stock and specially geared to run at speeds of up to 90 mph. *R. C. Riley/BM*

South London Line

FACTORY JUNCTION: It was to serve the new suburbs of Brixton, Peckham Rye and Denmark Hill that the LB&SCR opened its South London line between Victoria and London Bridge on 1 August 1865. With a train from Victoria to London Bridge at Wandsworth Road station in the background, Class 'C' 0-6-0 No 31690 negotiates the junction on 27 March 1957 with a small load of milk empties from Morden South to Bollo Lane.

The railway is still in operation today, providing a Monday-to-Saturday half-hour service, although yesterday's suburbs are generally considered as today's inner city. Unfortunately the old signal box window through which Dick Riley took his photograph is now plated up, and another window which provides a slightly different angle had to be used for the present scene. With the roof lights of the building beneath replaced with corrugated iron, the semaphore signals superseded by colour lights, and Wandsworth Road station in the background sporting a new footbridge, Class '73/1' electro-diesel No 73135 passes the same position on 2 May 1990, heading for Stewarts Lane depot with a defective coach that required attention. *R. C. Riley/KB*

CLAPHAM HIGH STREET: On 11 October 1953 a particularly ancient-looking 2NOL EMU, No 1803, restarts from what was then known as Clapham station, with a South London Line train for London Bridge. Introduced in 1934, these two-car units were actually made up from converted LSWR steam stock of much earlier vintage. At this time the station appeared in a reasonable state of repair and sported a platform canopy on the Victoria side as well as its own signal box and attendant semaphores.

By the late 1980s, as seen in the second view, Clapham station was in a particularly run-down condition, with the platform buildings seemingly derelict and held up by scaffolding, and corrugated iron covering the windows on the exit from the dank platform subway. It was no surprise when the station received media attention as the most ill-kept on Network SouthEast!

As indicated by the third view, taken in April 1989, NSE was stung into action by the adverse publicity and the station was soon to be smartened up considerably. By 1991-92 even the South London Line trains themselves were formed mainly of modern Class '456' stock. Now called Clapham High Street station, a particularly marked contrast with the earlier views is provided by new Class '456' EMU No 456024 forming the 09.52 service from Victoria to London Bridge on 4 April 1992. Passing on the ex-LC&DR main line alongside, a Class '415' 4EPB forms the 09.56 train from Victoria to Beckenham Junction. *R. C. Riley/KB/BM*

BRIXTON JUNCTION: Hauling empty coaching stock from Stewarts Lane, Ivatt Class '2MT' 2-6-2T No 41292 passes Brixton Junction on 8 May 1954, heading for Cannon Street.

Half-hourly Victoria-Orpington trains call at Brixton today, but since the closure of East Brixton station in January 1976 it is now bypassed by the South London Line, which crosses above on a recently rebuilt viaduct. Forming a Victoria-Margate service, routed through Catford and Canterbury West, Class '411/5' 4CEP No 1611 passes the same spot on 24 April 1989. Both the Bon Marche and Marks & Spencer buildings are still evident, but Brixton Junction signal box and signal gantry have disappeared. The brick wall on the right has sensibly been surmounted by railings, and the wall on the left has been completely renewed, and provides a walkway to help safeguard the well-being of track maintenance staff. *R. C. Riley/KB*

Surrey Suburbs

COULSDON: Opened in 1899 and originally called Stoats Nest, Coulsdon North station closed on 1 October 1983 with services being diverted to Smitham. With the junction to the station in course of being taken out, but with the signal box still in situ, Class '421/2' 4CIG No 7392 heads a Victoria-Hove-Littlehampton service, via the Quarry Line, on 26 January 1984.

Today no trace remains of the junction or the old box as the 15.30 Victoria-Gatwick Airport 'Gatwick Express' passes, powered by Class '73/2' No 73208 *Croydon 1883-1983*. Travelling in the opposite direction towards Victoria is an 8CIG formation with Class '421/2' No 1258 bringing up the rear. *BM/KB*

SUTTON: The route from West Croydon to Epsom brought Sutton its first trains in 1847, with the Epsom Downs branch following in 1865, and the line from Peckham Rye arriving in 1868. Finally the Southern Railway's line from Wimbledon came into use on 5 January 1930. Formed of a Class '405/2' 4SUB EMU, the 15.52 local service from Horsham to Victoria approaches the Sutton station stop on 5 April 1982.

Still situated at the junction of five lines, today's Sutton commuters enjoy 'South London Lines' trains from London Bridge via Mitcham Junction or West Croydon, services from Victoria to Epsom Downs or Horsham, and can also travel to Guildford or Luton on 'Thameslink'. With both 1982's motive power and signalling already history, the 12.20 Guildford-Luton 'Thameslink' service approaches, as the 12.16 London Bridge-Epsom train departs. The EMUs involved are, respectively, Class '319/0' No 319052 and Class '415/4' 4EPB No 5418. *Both BM*

VC
937

60

20

LIMIT
OF
SHUNT

EPSOM DOWNS (I): The LB&SCR branch to Epsom Downs was opened from Sutton to a terminus about three-quarters of a mile from Epsom Racecourse in May 1865; the branch was electrified in 1928. On 25 March 1980 the 15.38 train from Victoria to Epsom Downs, formed of Class '405/1' 4SUB EMUs Nos 4681 and 4721, passes the terminus signal box as it arrives at the end of its journey.

In 1989 the station was moved some 300 yards north of its former position and a completely new terminus was constructed as part of a new housing estate, the style of the station building being entirely sympathetic to the surrounding houses. The previous four platforms were reduced to one, which accommodates a half-hourly service from Victoria. Taken from the same position on 23 June 1990, the photograph shows a Class '455/8' unit No 5802 awaiting departure as the 09.43 to Victoria. *Both BM*

EPSOM DOWNS (2): The same train seen in the 1980 photograph opposite stands in platform 1 of the old station with the grass-overgrown outer platforms out of use but still visible to left and right, a relic of once-hectic Epsom race days.

A road through the housing estate to the new station now stands where the island platform used to be, demolition of the 1865 LB&SCR station having taken place rapidly on 15-16 February 1989. *Both BM*

TATTENHAM CORNER: Constructed by the SE&CR into the heartlands of the LB&SCR, the branch line from Tadworth to the Tattenham Corner of Epsom Downs racecourse was opened on Derby Day 1901 in open and unashamed competition with its rival. Built right beside the racecourse, the six-platform terminus had more convenient and spacious facilities than Epsom Downs station, and when race traffic was at its peak in the 1920s and 1930s some 60 specials ran to Tattenham Corner on Derby Day, including the Royal Train. After this the need for race specials dwindled as a result of lower race attendances, coupled with increased car ownership. Other than on race days, the present train service outside the rush hours is hourly from Victoria. On 25 March 1980 Class '415/1' 4EPB No 5002 and Class '416/1' 2EPB No 5652 stand at the buffer-stops awaiting their duties.

Currently the station has been smartened up by NSE, and has had modern platform lighting installed. Otherwise the terminus looks very much the same, as Class '455/8' No 5829 awaits departure as the 11.15 service to Victoria, via Purley and East Croydon, a journey scheduled to take 54 minutes. *Both BM*

Euston

EUSTON (I): The London & Birmingham was the first trunk railway in the world. Other lines came into being prior to its 1837 opening, but the London & Birmingham Railway was considered as the greatest railway event of its kind. From early beginnings its London terminus of Euston developed into a rather sprawling and untidy 15-platform station, which was set back off the Euston Road behind the Euston Hotel and the rather grand Doric arch gateway that led to Hardwick's Great Hall of 1849. The original terminus at the foot of Camden bank was gradually swallowed up by the expanding needs of the LNWR until just the hotel, Doric arch and Great Hall survived. At the buffer-stops of platforms 1 and 2 of the old Euston, 'Jubilee' Class 4-6-0 No 45637 *Windward Islands* and original 'Royal Scot' 4-6-0 No 46134 *The Cheshire Regiment* stand with morning arrivals on 1 June 1951.

The remaining landmarks of the old Euston were completely swept away during the construction of the present-day Euston station, opened in October 1968. At platform 2 on 1 April 1992 the 10.30 Intercity service from Manchester Piccadilly has just arrived, headed by non-powered Driving Van Trailer (DVT) No 82131. The locomotive which has provided power for the journey is on the other end of the train. *Both BM*

EUSTON (2): Rebuilt 'Royal Scot' 4-6-0 No 46164 *The Artists' Rifleman* arrives at Euston on 21 August 1951 with the 'Manxman' express from Liverpool Lime Street, so called as it connected with the Isle of Man ferry.

The Euston of today is certainly modern, but to that doubtful epithet must be added the words cold and inhospitable. At the time of the rebuilding considerable pressure was brought to bear upon British Rail to prevent the wholesale destruction of every vestige of the old Euston, including the famous Doric arch, but all to no avail. Under the present-day airport-style structure, the 10.10 Intercity train from Liverpool Lime Street stands in the same position on 1 April 1992, having been brought in by Class '86/1' No 86101 *Sir William A. Stanier FRS* which, instead of propelling the train from the rear, has had to tow its DVT No 82121 as result of a faulty connection with the control wiring through the train. *Both BM*

EUSTON (3): At the 'country end' of Euston station on 3 August 1958 Stanier Class '8F' 2-8-0 No 48122 prepares to haul the ECS of the 'Mancunian' express away to Stonebridge Park carriage depot for servicing, a depot constructed in 1953 to supersede the old Willesden Junction carriage sheds. To the rear, departing from platform 4, is one of the LNWR 'Oerlikon' EMUs dating from 1915 and forming a stopping train for Watford Junction.

Departing from the same platform at the Euston of today, Class '86/2' No 86222 *Lloyd's List 250th Anniversary* removes ECS of the 09.29 service from Carlisle, which it is taking to the carriage depot at Stonebridge Park, now given the rather grand title of Wembley Intercity Depot. *Both BM*

Camden Bank

CAMDEN BANK (I): Trains depart from Euston on a down gradient of 1 in 149, levelling to 1 in 575 before coming to the foot of Camden Bank, where a testing assault of 1 in 70 prevails for nearly a mile to the summit at 1 in 77. In steam days locomotives climbing the hill with the heavier expresses often made an impressive sight with wheelslip causing spectacular exhausts. Approaching Camden summit, an unusual sight on 21 September 1958 was Thompson Class 'L1' 2-6-4T No 67747 hauling ECS for Stonebridge Park carriage sheds. The Eastern Region locomotive was allocated to Neasden shed (see page 80), which as 34E came under the auspices of King's Cross (34A). However, Neasden was transferred to the London Midland Region in 1958, and became 14D under Cricklewood. Most of the Eastern Region locomotives were soon to be transferred away, but this one remained long enough to receive a 14D smokebox shed-plate, and thus found itself working a duty of this type out of Euston.

Passing the same spot in 1990 Class '321/4' EMU No 321426 forms a semi-fast service from Euston to Milton Keynes. The background has changed out of all recognition, and the underbridge has disappeared. The siding on the right has disappeared, but the 'section gap' notice remains in situ on the left. *R. C. Riley/KB*

109

CAMDEN BANK (2): With a warm autumn sun dissipating the best of the exhaust effect from the chimney, Riddles Standard Class '7MT' 'Pacific' No 70033 *Charles Dickens* hammers up the Bank on 7 October 1958 hauling all-maroon stock forming an express for Manchester (London Road).

Camden bank offers few problems to the electric locomotive-hauled expresses of today, although it is not unknown even for these to suffer wheelslip when rails become wet and greasy. On a very dull but dry morning Class 86/2 No 86233 *Laurence Olivier* climbs the bank without fuss, hauling the 08.20 Intercity service from Euston to Blackpool North. Apart from the obvious accoutrements of the overhead electrification and a much enlarged tree, Camden Bank remains little changed over the years. *Both BM*

Camden (1B)

CAMDEN SHED (I): Major engineering features of the newly-opened London & Birmingham Railway included the great 'Engine House' containing the Camden Bank winding engines and the nearby engine shed. By 1844 locomotives were found to be capable of climbing the Bank unaided and the stationary engines were dispensed with. Locomotive servicing facilities remained, however, with two new sheds being constructed in 1847, one for goods engines on the original site on the east side of the line, and the other for passenger locomotives on the west side. This latter shed was greatly altered and modernised by the LMS and is shown here, as Camden (1B), being passed by 'Patriot' Class '6P' 4-6-0 No 45516 *The Bedfordshire and Hertfordshire Regiment* hauling the 16.47 train from Euston to Northampton and Stafford. The two personages taking photographs on the shed during an official visit by the Railway Photographic Society on 16 July 1958 are Geoff Rixon and, with inevitable tripod, Maurice Earley.

After a spell as a diesel depot from 1962, Camden 'top link' closed in 1966, and the site is now completely taken over by carriage sidings where, on 22 April 1992, a Class '321/4' EMU is being passed by the 15.30 Euston-Crewe Parcels train hauled by 'Rail Express Services' (RES) Class '86/4' No 86401, a locomotive once painted in NSE colours and named *Northampton Town*. *Both BM*

CAMDEN SHED (2): Camden Shed's 70-foot vacuum-operated turntable was installed by the LMS in 1936, replacing a 60-foot turntable which in turn had replaced a 35-foot one installed in 1870. On 16 July 1958 'Patriot' 4-6-0 No 45546 *Fleetwood* is turned ready to back down for 'coaling up' at the coaling plant behind.

The site from the same viewpoint in April 1992 shows a line-up of Class '321/4' EMUs awaiting the evening rush hour, headed by No 321427. The background buildings on the right remain, although their previously blank walls have had windows built in. *Both BM*

CAMDEN SHED (3): In pristine red livery, 'Princess Royal' Class '8P' 'Pacific' No 46200 *The Princess Royal* is turned on the Camden turntable on the same day, in readiness to back down to Euston and take out one of the crack West Coast Main Line expresses of the day.

In 1992 a Class '321/4' rests at the extremity of the present-day Camden sidings in the position where the turntable used to be situated. The buildings at the rear are obviously the same ones which were in the background 34 years before, although they do show a number of alterations which have occurred during the passage of time. *Both BM*

CAMDEN ROUNDHOUSE: Constructed in 1847 on the site of the original London & Birmingham Railway engine shed of 1837, the now-famous 'Roundhouse' in Chalk Farm Road, London NW3, was brick-built to a diameter of 160 feet, and had 24 roads radiating out from a 35-foot centre turntable. As was noted earlier, it was built as a maintenance shed for freight locomotives, with the site on the opposite side of the line being constructed at the same time for passenger types, and surviving to become Camden (1B). The 'Roundhouse', however, was last utilised for railway purposes in 1871, and was leased by the railway to W. & A. Gilbey who used it to store their well-known brand of gin until the listed structure was handed over to the arts in 1964, after which it was used as a theatre. Presently the old building is boarded up, and awaiting a decision as to its future use. Passing the 145-year-old structure on 3 October 1959 with a container freight that could be considered as a forerunner to today's 'Freightliner' workings, Stanier 'Black Five' mixed traffic 4-6-0 No 45111 awaits a clear signal to proceed through Primrose Hill station on the North London Line route to continue its journey northward.

Seen from the same viewpoint on 22 April 1992 Class '90/1' No 90134 passes in the opposite direction with a 'Freightliner' bound for Felixstowe. *R. C. Riley/BM*

CAMDEN SUMMIT: Southwards from Tring, the West Coast route is relatively flat until Camden Bank is reached a mile out of Euston, when trains go 'over the top' to descend into the terminus. Drifting easily down the first part of the bank at 1 in 77, rebuilt 'Patriot' 4-6-0 No 45545 *Planet* heads an express from Wolverhampton on 3 August 1958.

On 22 April 1992 RES-liveried Class '90/0' No 90020 *Colonel Bill Cockburn CBE TD* passes the same location heading for Euston with the 06.30 Parcels service from Glasgow Polmadie. *Both BM*

PRIMROSE HILL TUNNEL: Just over 1¼ miles from its Euston destination, the 'Emerald Isle Express' from Holyhead bursts from the depths of Primrose Hill tunnel on 6 June 1973, powered by Class '86' No E3106 (now No 86214 *Sans Pareil*).

Mk III DVT No 82152 emerges from the tunnel at the same position on 22 April 1992 heading the 12.55 Wolverhampton-Euston Intercity service, which has Class '86/2' No 86225 *Hardwicke* out of sight in the tunnel providing the necessary traction. A new-style speed restriction sign is in place, and the building above the tunnel has been truncated. The tunnel brickwork itself has been nicely cleaned up. *Both BM*

Willesden (1A)

WILLESDEN SHED: To attend to the needs of their freight locomotives, many railway companies with a London terminus found it necessary to construct an engine shed on the nearest available land outside the capital. To ease pressure on Camden shed, Willesden depot was constructed by the LNWR in 1873 for this purpose and, coded 1A in 1935, was always primarily a freight depot. A view of the shed taken from across the Grand Union Canal *circa* 1936 shows early 'Black Fives', Class '4F' 0-6-0s and 'Jinties' all simmering outside the original 12-road straight shed, a structure substantially unchanged since it was built, although extended in 1898 to enlarge its capacity; the two types of architecture are clearly apparent, and give the building a somewhat hybrid appearance. Willesden-allocated steam engines continued to soldier on powering freights and the like during the advent of dieselisation, but electrification finally rendered the depot redundant; it was closed in September 1965 and afterwards demolished, the site being taken over by the Willesden 'Freightliner' terminal.

From the same position in 1992 it can be seen that a bridge has been constructed across the canal to connect the terminal with the adjacent freight lines, and on the skyline can be seen the variety of prefabricated buildings which have replaced 1A. The present-day Willesden Traction Depot, constructed to maintain the current fleet of electric locomotives, is situated on the other side of the main line. *Lens of Sutton/BM*

Into Middlesex and Herts

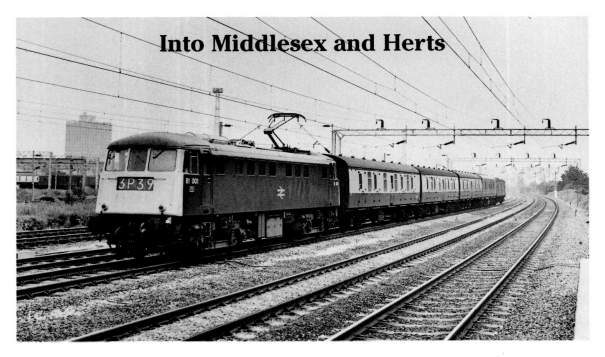

WEMBLEY: Apart from the main line itself, the route between Willesden and Wembley Central has always been bordered by extensive sidings and depots throughout its length, variously referred to as Willesden, Stonebridge Park, Brent, Wembley and, latterly, Wembley International Freight Yard. Nearing Wembley Central station on 26 June 1973, the first electric locomotive constructed for the WCML electrification, Class '81' No 81001, heads a Euston-Carlisle District parcels train.

Passing the yards under construction for Channel Tunnel freight traffic at the same place on 11 April 1992, Class '321/4' EMU No 321440 forms the 16.54 semi-fast service from Euston to Birmingham New Street. *Both BM*

SOUTH KENTON: Passing the Middlesex suburbs of South Kenton on 29 August 1964, a fitted freight from Willesden heads northwards in the hands of Stanier 'Black Five' 4-6-0 No 44680.

At the same location just over 15 years later very little appears to have changed apart from the tree growth as Class '85' No 85030 accelerates north with the 12.43 'Silcock & Collins Express' of covered 'cartics'. The train has begun its journey from the Ford Motor Company plant sidings at Dagenham Dock, with Liverpool Garston as its destination. All the first-generation WCML electric locomotives of Classes '81' to '85' have now been withdrawn from service. *P. J. Lynch/BM*

BUSHEY TROUGHS (I): Despite Nationalisation having taken place some three years earlier, the legend 'LMS' still appears on the tender of unrebuilt 'Royal Scot' 4-6-0 No 46110 *Grenadier Guardsman* on 19 May 1951 as the locomotive scoops up a little too much water from Bushey troughs on the way northwards with an express from Euston to Llandudno and Holyhead.

Modern electric traction has no need of water troughs. With those at Bushey having been taken out in the 1960s, the 15.00 Intercity express from Euston to Birmingham New Street passes the site on 11 April 1992 powered by as yet un-named Class '90' No 90003. *Both BM*

BUSHEY TROUGHS (2): Seen from the same vantage point as the view on the previous pages, but with the camera pointing in the opposite direction, 'Princess Royal' 'Pacific' No 46207 *Princess Arthur of Connaught* has no need of water replenishment while passing over Bushey troughs on 25 March 1953 with a Euston-bound express from Scotland.

Passing the same four-arch bridge on 11 April 1992, the 13.48 express from Birmingham New Street has 16 miles to travel before coming to rest at the Euston buffer-stops. Leading the train is Mk III DVT No 82138, while providing traction and propelling from the rear is Class '87/0' No 87025 *County of Cheshire*. *Both BM*

BUSHEY: Between Bushey station (or Bushey & Oxhey as it was then called) and the troughs once stood the large water-softening tower which supplied water to the pick-up channels. Passing the building on the same day in 1953 ex-LNWR Class 'G2a' 0-8-0 No 49450 trundles towards London hauling wooden-sided coal wagons.

Scurrying past the same position on 11 April 1992, a Milton Keynes-Euston semi-fast service is in the hands of Class '321/4' EMU No 321431. The water tower has gone together with the centre road siding, modern flat-bottom track has replaced the old bullhead variety, and the embankment has become an almost impenetrable woodland. *Both BM*

WATFORD JUNCTION (I): Hauling the 15 coaches of the 10.40 Euston-Carlisle express, 'Princess Coronation' Class '8P' 'Pacific' No 46229 *Duchess of Hamilton* (now preserved as part of the National Collection and still working on the main line today) hammers past Watford No 1 signal box on a wet 9 August 1952.

On 11 April 1992 the 12.00 Euston-Wolverhampton Intercity express rushes through Watford and passes the same position, unusually powered by a pair of Class '86/2' electric locomotives, No 86210 *City of Edinburgh* and No 86258 *Talyllyn - The First Preserved Railway*. The signal box and semaphore signals have been superseded by Watford power box (out of the picture to the right) and colour light signals, one of the two nearside tracks has been removed, and lineside electrical boxes and overhead catenary masts now clutter the scene. In fact, all that seems to have visibly improved is the weather! *Both BM*

WATFORD JUNCTION (2): Watford is designated as a junction because of the branch line to St Albans Abbey station, a distance of 6¼ miles. In August 1952 the branch service was being operated by ACV demonstration railcars Nos 1, 2 and 3, seen here forming the 17.48 to Abbey station alongside a Class '7F' 'G2a' 0-8-0 No 49145 which is coming off shed in order to take out a freight for Bescot from the adjacent yards.

The bay platform for St Albans Abbey trains, together with the site of Watford shed (1C), is now a car park, and the through line on the other side of the platform is now used for the branch trains which were in the hands of Class '313' EMUS from electrification in July 1988, but are now operated by Class '321s'. On 11 April 1992 unit No 321428 was operating the 'Abbey Flyer' shuttle, and can just be seen over the fence, having discharged its passengers after arrival as the 13.30 from St Albans, returning from Watford as the 13.50. *Both BM*

WATFORD CUTTING (I): Manchester Longsight-allocated Class '5MT' 'Crab' 2-6-0 No 42887 snakes around the curves of the WCML slow lines south of Watford tunnel on 9 August 1952, hauling a fitted freight of impressive length bound for Willesden.

At the same location on 11 April 1992 the 09.10 Intercity service from Liverpool Lime Street to Euston is headed by Mk III DVT No 82131, with Class '86/1' No 86101 *Sir William A. Stanier FRS* providing traction, propelling out of sight at the rear. The DVT has its usual sleek front-end appearance slightly marred by one jumper cable cover being in the raised position with the other one correctly closed. Apart from the trappings of electrification, Watford cutting has changed little over the years. *Both BM*

WATFORD CUTTING (2): Bursting from the southern portal of Watford tunnel on 9 August 1952 'Royal Scot' Class '7P' 4-6-0 No 46135 *The East Lancashire Regiment* approaches Watford on the fast line with the 'Merseyside Express' from Liverpool Lime Street incorporating through coaches from Southport.

On 11 April 1992 the 09.36 'Little Euston' semi-fast service from Birmingham New Street to Euston is seen at the same place, formed of Class '321/4' EMU No 321440. *Both BM*

St Pancras

ST PANCRAS (1): The Midland Railway opened its London terminus at the eastern end of the Euston Road in 1868 and it took its name from the parish in which it was constructed. For nearly a century the train shed, engineerd by W. H. Barlow, had the largest station roof in the world without internal supports. Giving some indication of dramatic Victorian engineering at its finest, the lofty single span overall roof provides a background to Stanier Class '3MT' 2-6-2T No 40172 on 3 August 1958 as it awaits to depart for Cricklewood sidings with the ECS of an earlier arrival from Leicester.

Although the early colour light signals and platform lighting have been updated, trackwork and platforms have been altered, and the accoutrements of overhead electrification intrude, the HSTs of today still look strangely out of place in the same setting. On 13 April 1992 'Intercity 125' services for Sheffield and Nottingham respectively await departure with Class '43' power cars Nos 43074 and 43083 leading. *Both BM*

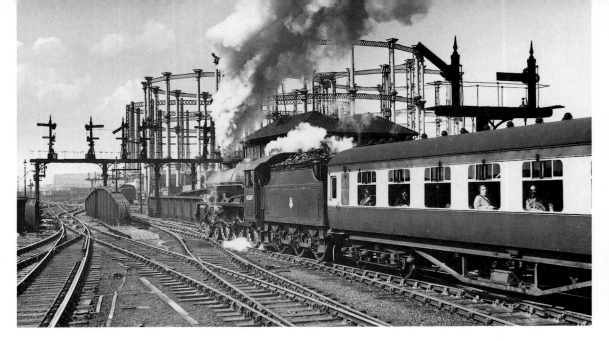

ST PANCRAS (2): Nearly as famous as the St Pancras train shed are the adjacent gas holders, some of which, like St Pancras station building, are the subject of a preservation order. On 14 May 1955 'Jubilee' Class '6P' 4-6-0 No 45589 *Gwalior* makes a smokey start from the old Midland terminus with the 16.15 train for Leeds and Bradford.

With an engineer's occupation near Wembley requiring services from Liverpool and Holyhead to use the facilities of St Pancras instead of Euston, Mk III DVT No 82112 departs on 13 October 1991 leading the 11.39 Intercity service to Liverpool Lime Street, powered from the rear by Class '87/0' No 87026 *Sir Richard Arkwright*. A lengthened platform has resulted in changes to the track layout, and the semaphore signalling has gone together with the most distant gas holder. *P. J. Lynch/BM*

CAMBRIDGE STREET DEPOT: Just as in the case of Ranelagh Bridge, Paddington (page 13), diesel locomotives arriving at St Pancras were able to avoid fuelling trips to Cricklewood by using the fuelling depot at Cambridge Street, a short way out from the terminus. Ranelagh Bridge was made redundant when the HSTs were introduced, and a few years later the same fate befell Cambridge Street. On 9 March 1978 Class '47/4' No 47491 and Class '45/1' 'Peak' No 45123 *The Lancashire Fusilier* attend for fuelling.

In April 1992 only the old buffer-stop remains as evidence that the depot ever existed. *Both BM*

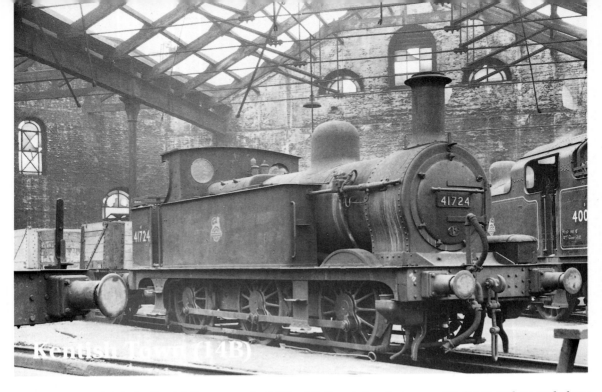

Kentish Town (14B)

KENTISH TOWN SHED (I): Kentish Town was the Midland Railway's London passenger depot, and opened along with the company's London extension to St Pancras in 1867-68. A number of alterations and enlargements were made at various times over the years and the shed was a busy one, as it not only had its own allocation of over 100 locomotives, but was also responsible for servicing the motive power arriving at St Pancras from other major depots such as Derby, Leicester, Nottingham and Sheffield. Dieselisation on the Midland main line, and in particular the advent of the Rolls Royce-engined Class '127' DMUs on local services, rendered the depot facilities redundant quite early, and closure came about in 1963. Standing inside 'No 1' shed, or the 'Metro' as it was better known, 1878 Johnson-designed ex-Midland Class '1F' 0-6-0T No 41724, used for shunting and local goods workings, poses for the camera on 19 December 1954. Following Second World War bomb damage, the roof here was eventually replaced in 1958.

The old 14B complex today is occupied by J. Murphy & Sons (Contractors) Ltd, to whom thanks are due for enabling the present-day comparision views to be taken. Both BM

KENTISH TOWN SHED (2): Until Cricklewood shed (14A) opened in 1882, Kentish Town was known simply as 'London'. On 15 June 1955 1911-designed Fowler Class '4F' 0-6-0 No 43964 stands outside the depot minus a connecting rod.

With the background chimney providing a reference point, the present-day view looks across the contractor's yard. *Both BM*

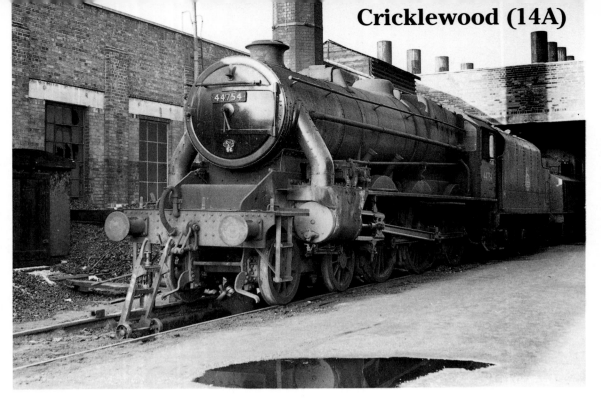

CRICKLEWOOD SHED: Following the opening of the Midland's London extension, sidings for freight sorting were laid outside the capital at Brent, and a small four-road shed, 'Hendon', was opened in 1870. This became inadequate for the company's burgeoning freight traffic, and a new roundhouse was constructed in 1882, known until the turn of the century as Childs Hill. In 1893 a second roundhouse was added, followed by a fitting shop and a number of other enlargements. Now known as Cricklewood, the depot had an allocation in the 1950s of over 80 engines, although these numbers had reduced considerably by the time a few of those from Kentish Town arrived after that shed closed. On 28 November 1954 one of seven Stanier 'Black Fives' fitted with Caprotti valve gear and Timken roller bearings, No 44754, stands outside the depot awaiting a return working home to Leeds Holbeck (20A).

Later a new diesel depot opened on the opposite side of the line, being known as Cricklewood East and assuming the mantle of 14A, the original complex becoming 14B Cricklewood West. Decreasing numbers of locomotives used the original facility, until steam was finally banished from the Midland line on 14 December 1964. Diesel traction used the premises as a stabling point for a time thereafter, but the buildings were eventually demolished and, as shown below, the site has now been taken over by a large Royal Mail 'Parcel Force' depot. *Both BM*

CRICKLEWOOD DIESEL DEPOT: Following the demise of Cricklewood West, the diesel depot became plain Cricklewood, and was responsible for maintaining both main-line and freight locomotives in addition to the DMU commuter fleet. On 29 October 1978 Class '45/0' 'Peaks' Nos 45065, 45077 and 45042 await their next duties alongside Class '25/2' No 25117.

Despite being relatively modern, this depot itself closed in 1987 following the electrification of the local services to Bedford and the main-line workings being taken over by HSTs. A building to stable EMUs was constructed a short distance down the line, but this had no official motive power allocation; it has now been taken over by Charterail Ltd. On 21 April 1992 the depot buildings still stand but are no longer in use. *Both BM*

The Midland Main Line

BRENT YARDS: With a long haul of coal wagons from the Midlands, BR Standard Class '9F' 2-10-0 No 92009 arrives at Brent Yards, Cricklewood, passing between Brent Junction No 1 and No 2 signal boxes on 19 March 1955. Two steel-sided wagons are next to the locomotive, but the rest of the rolling-stock still consists of much older wooden-bodied vehicles.

Although rationalised and reduced in area, the yards at Brent are still important for today's transfer freight. Passing the same location on 4 May 1990, Class '319/0' 'Thameslink' units Nos 319032 and 319019 glide past heading away from the camera, forming the 18.52 service from St Pancras to Bedford. *R. C. Riley/BM*

HENDON: Passing Hendon on the same day in 1955, another Riddles-designed BR Standard '9F' 2-10-0 heads for Brent Yards with a similar haul of coal from Toton Yards. This train has a few more steel wagons interspersed among the wooden ones than the example opposite, and the locomotive itself, No 92045, is a later one with a more modern Type BR1C tender.

Embankment foliage prevents an exactly similar angle being obtained for a present-day view. However, at the same location on 16 May 1990 a test train from Derby Research & Technical Centre heads southwards, hauled by one of the Research Centre's own allocated Class '47/4' locomotives, No 47973 (since named *Derby Evening Telegraph*). The location is much the same as in the past, although the bridge spanning Hendon station has been modified to allow for the installation of the overhead electrification catenary. *R. C. Riley/KB*

SILKSTREAM JUNCTION: Situated just north of Hendon, Silkstream Junction originally marked the bifurcation of the southbound slow lines into Local and Goods lines, the latter passing over the down Local and up and down Fast lines by a flyover to form six running lines between here and Finchley Road. With the junction signal box in the distance, a St Albans-St Pancras stopping train takes the up Local and heads for the Hendon stop on 25 May 1957, hauled by Fairburn Class '4MT' 2-6-4T No 42178.

Forming the 11.37 Bedford-Brighton 'Thameslink' service on 18 September 1988, Class '319' No 319055 passes the once rural-looking scene. Behind the fencing today is the M1 motorway! *Both BM*

MILL HILL BROADWAY: Pulling away from the Mill Hill Broadway stop on 25 May 1957, Fairburn Class '4MT' 2-6-4T No 42680 hauls the 16.40 local train from St Pancras to St Albans.

With the northbound carriageway of the M1 motorway now running through where the background houses used to be, Class '319/0' 'Thameslink' EMU No 319057 restarts the 11.20 Guildford-Luton train away from the station, as the rear of a train of empty spoil wagons from Forders Sidings, Stewartby, to Chatham Dockyard can be seen proceeding in the opposite direction. *Both BM*

ELSTREE & BOREHAMWOOD (I): Although the Beyer-Garratt type of locomotive was very successful in Africa, it found little demand in its British homeland. The LNER had one, but the only others in main-line use within these shores were the 33 2-6-6-2Ts which worked Toton-Brent coal trains for some 30 years. Approaching Elstree tunnel on the up slow line from the north on 12 April 1952, No 47994 heads a typical coal train of the day and passes under the boxed-in sewage outlet pipe that once crossed the tracks here.

With the pipe now removed to make way for the overhead electrification catenary, Class '56' No 56057 passes the same spot on 13 April 1992, hauling a Shanks & McEwan train of empty household waste containers, returning to their Cricklewood Depot from the landfill site at Forders Sidings, near Stewartby, in Bedfordshire. *Both BM*

ELSTREE & BOREHAMWOOD (2): On the same day in 1952 'Jubilee' Class 4-6-0 No 45568 *Western Australia* hammers through the down fast line cutting away from Elstree tunnel hauling the 'Thames-Clyde Express' from St Pancras to Glasgow St Enoch.

Embankment foliage looks to be getting out of hand as the 11.30 St Pancras-Nottingham HST charges past on 13 April 1992, headed by Class '43' power car No 43056 with its *University of Bradford* nameplates missing. *Both BM*

ELSTREE TUNNEL: Taking trains beneath the South Herts plateau, the twin-bore Elstree tunnel was a major engineering accomplishment required for the Midland Railway to achieve its 'London Extension' of 1868. On 25 May 1957 BR Standard Class '9F' 2-10-0 No 92058 emerges from the fast line tunnel with a Toton-bound coal train from Brent.

At the same location on 13 April 1992 Class '319/1' 'Thameslink' EMU No 319171 emerges from the 1,058-yard bore forming the 09.30 Brighton-Bedford train. *Both BM*

King's Cross

KING'S CROSS (1): Designed by Lewis Cubitt and constructed on the site of the London Smallpox Hospital, King's Cross station opened in 1852, its two great round-arched train sheds once being used, respectively, for train arrivals and departures. Apart from electrification, track rationalisation and the number of engine-spotters about, very little has changed in the 37 years that separate these particular views. (Above) On 5 July 1952, Peppercorn Class 'A1' 'Pacific' No 60122 *Curlew* awaits departure time with the 'Aberdonian' express. (Below) On 23 July 1989, Class '317/2' EMU No 317351 is stabled in the Network SouthEast suburban platforms awaiting the evening commuters while, under the station roof, InterCity 125 HSTs await their respective departure times, forming the 15.00 to Glasgow Queen Street and the 15.32 to Edinburgh. *Both BM*

KING'S CROSS (2): British Rail staff gave permission for some 40 parcels trolleys to be moved out of the way in order to copy this view of Platform 1 at King's Cross but, wisely, did not offer any assistance! (Above) On 11 January 1952, Thompson Class 'L1' 2-6-4T No 67745 prepares to haul the 18.25 semi-fast train to Baldock. Showing that the platform has been significantly widened, the second view, taken on 27 November 1988, shows Class '317/2' EMU No 317365 forming the 15.45 service to Cambridge. *BM/KB*

KING'S CROSS (3): The once classic view of King's Cross station from atop Gasworks Tunnel was ruined when unsightly girders were erected from which to suspend the overhead electric wiring; similar electrification at next-door St Pancras station has been accomplished in a much less heavy-handed fashion. (Left) Forming the 14.30 to Leeds, an InterCity 125 HST with Class '43' power car No 43074 leading, draws away from the station on 4 February 1989. (Below) In June 1975, aesthetically happier days, Class '55' 'Deltic' No 55007 *Pinza* passes the old signal box with the 10.20 Intercity train for Leeds while two trains of empty coaching stock wait to leave, both powered by Class '31/1' diesels. *Both BM*

KING'S CROSS (4): The contrast between the old, musty King's Cross suburban platforms of Eastern Region and those of the bright, new-look Network SouthEast Sector of the present day must have a lot to do with the resurgence of commuter travel from the station. During the intervening years between these two photographs of platforms 9, 10 and 11, the latter, on the right, has been filled in and dug out again, business having first slackened and then returned to buoyancy. The above view shows a somewhat drab November day in 1972 with two Rolls Royce-engined Class '125' DMUs awaiting departure with respective services for Welwyn Garden City and Hertford North. The present-day view, below, taken on the morning of 21 January 1989, shows Class '317/1' No 317347 forming the 08.40 to Royston, and Class '317/2' No 317365 with a later departure for Hertford North. Both units are painted in the distinctive NSE livery of red, white, blue and grey. *Brian Beer/BM*

KING'S CROSS SHED (2): The 70 ft high reinforced concrete coaling plant at 34A was similar to many others constructed for the LNER in the late 1920s and early 1930s and had a 500-ton bunker capacity. On 9 May 1954, Class 'A2' 'Pacific' No 60513 *Dante* fills its tender. On 10 September 1989, nothing remains to show that the concrete monolith ever existed. *BM/KB*

Great Northern suburbs

FINSBURY PARK: The track layout has changed quite considerably, the station sidings are no more and No 5 signal box has been demolished. The houses in the background remain (albeit rather obscured by advancing greenery), and the small brick-built container in the foreground, once used for junk, now makes an attempt to resemble a garden plant box. Just 17 years separate these two views of the northern approaches to Finsbury Park station, with the January 1972 one (above) showing Class '31/1' No 5545 hauling a southbound ballast train and, in the same position on 23 July 1989, Class '43' InterCity 125 power car No 43089 beginning to slow for the final lap into King's Cross, fronting the 07.25 HST from Newcastle. *Brian Beer/KB*

FINSBURY PARK DEPOT: Following the elimination of steam locomotive working in the King's Cross area and the subsequent closure of Top Shed (34A), the country's first purpose-built diesel maintenance depot was constructed in 1960 in Clarence Yard goods depot on the west side of the Great Northern main line south of Finsbury Park station. It was given responsibility for the maintenance of both main-line diesel-electric locomotives and a fleet of diesel shunters. On 15 January 1977 we see just two of the locomotives allocated to the depot, Class '55' 'Deltic' No 55007 *Pinza* and Class '08' shunter No 08551.

Finsbury Park depot finally went out of use on 3 October 1983 following the introduction of InterCity 125 High Speed Trains, the maintenance of which in the King's Cross area is undertaken at Bounds Green depot, near Alexandra Palace station. On 27 July 1989 the depot was still standing, although a combination of vandalism and the elements had taken their toll. It has since been demolished to make way for new flats. *Both BM*

HARRINGAY: (Above) On 15 July 1952, the 'Harrogate Sunday Pullman' titled train rounds the curve approaching Harringay station powered by Class 'A1' 'Pacific' No 60139 *Sea Eagle.* Today, the tracks are banked for high speed running, electricity abounds, in the shape of both catenary and signalling, and the down line is now the up! (Below) Propelling its Mk 3 train towards the capital on 25 May 1989, Class '91' No 91003 powers the 16.10 Leeds–King's Cross. *Both BM*

HORNSEY SHED: Primarily responsible for the Eastern Region's Great Northern line London allocation of smaller freight locomotives, Hornsey shed (34B) closed to steam traction in 1961. Without the roof ventilators, the building survives to the present time and is used as a store for the nearby Hornsey electric depot. (Above) On 3 October 1954, one of Hornsey's prolific allocation of Class 'N1' 0-6-2Ts, No 69455, stands alongside a Gresley Class 'J50/2' 0-6-0T No 68931. The view below shows how the structure looked in July 1989. *Both BM*

WOOD GREEN/ALEXANDRA PALACE: (Above) Passing through Wood Green station on 19 July 1952, a southbound fitted freight nears its destination of King's Cross Goods, uncommonly headed by Gresley Class 'A4' 'Pacific' No 60010 *Dominion of Canada*. Apart from the station name changing from Wood Green to Alexandra Palace, the present-day scene is still similar in a number of respects, although the footbridge nearest to the camera has been taken down and the other replaced with a metal structure, the old station canopies have gone and, of course, the ugly accessories to overhead electrification are everywhere. (Below) On 17 February 1989, Class '43' InterCity 125 power car No 43039 hares through the station with the 06.55 HST from Edinburgh to King's Cross. *BM/KB*

WOOD GREEN FLYOVER: The six tracks in existence in the 27 March 1954 view (above) had been reduced to four when the comparison photograph was taken on 3 June 1989, but apart from the flyover having been raised to provide the required clearance for the overhead electrified wiring, all else appears unchanged except for the motive power. In the 1950s view, Class 'A1' 'Pacific' No 60120 *Kittiwake* hauls the 13.05 King's Cross–Bradford express. The HST (below) is led by Class '43' power car No 43095 *Heaton* and is the 19.00 King's Cross–Newcastle Intercity service. *BM/KB*

WOOD GREEN TUNNEL: A gap of 35 years separates these two views of freight trains emerging from Wood Green Tunnel. The raised track on which 'WD' Class 2-8-0 No 90554 is travelling on 27 March 1954 (above) was later lowered to allow for electrification work to take place inside the tunnel, and trees and shrubs now abound on the bank and above the tunnel mouth, obscuring most of the houses which, previously, had an uninterrupted view of the East Coast Main Line. Heading southwards, hauling a variety of old wooden-sided wagons, the steam age photograph provides a contrast to the more modern image of the Railfreight Distribution Sector Class '37/0' locomotives with a haul of tanks making up the 13.10 train from Kilnhurst to Ripple Lane, Barking, on 27 July 1989 (below). The leading locomotive is No 37272 which is working in multiple with No 37059 *Port of Tilbury. Both BM*

OAKLEIGH PARK: Apart from the advent of electrification and the removal of the signal box, the environs of Oakleigh Park station would appear to have changed remarkably little in the 36 years which separate these identical viewpoints; the background poplar trees have grown to an expected extent but the two larger trees have changed not at all. (Above) On 28 February 1953, Class 'J50/3' 0-6-0T No 68968 steams through Oakleigh Park with an up freight for Hornsey. (Below) On 27 July 1989, Class '313' EMU No 313054 travels the same route, forming the 19.51 local service from Welwyn Garden City to Moorgate. *Both BM*

HADLEY WOOD: (Above) Formed of two Gresley four-car articulated 'Quadart' sets, the 18.25 King's Cross–Welwyn Garden City local service is restarted from the Hadley Wood stop on 1 July 1952 by Gresley Class 'N2/4' 0-6-2T No 69586. Shortly after this photograph was taken, Government authority was at last obtained (nothing changes!) for work to commence on opening up the tunnels on the $2^{1}/_{2}$-mile stretch of line between New Barnet and Potters Bar to enable additional up and down tracks to be laid in order to alleviate that major bottleneck on the Great Northern route. Both Hadley Wood and Potters Bar stations were modernised, with four platforms, and the works were not completed until May 1959. Following the first stage of electrification, the July 1979 view (below) shows Class '312' and '313' EMUs forming, respectively, a King's Cross–Royston semi-fast train and a Moorgate–Welwyn Garden City service. *Both BM*

HADLEY WOOD NORTH TUNNEL: Track maintenance personnel were plain 'gangers' when the above photograph was taken, on Sunday 13 July 1952, of Thompson Class 'B1' 4-6-0 No 61027 *Madoqua* ambling away from Hadley Wood North Tunnel with an up freight for King's Cross Goods. (Below) On 4 November 1989, Class '317/1' EMU No 317345 is travelling very much faster, forming the 14.10 train from Cambridge to King's Cross. Four tracks, electrification and colour light signalling are now apparent at this previously rural setting. *Both BM*

POTTERS BAR (1): (Above) Prior to the East Coast Main Line widening that took place during the 1950s, Gresley Class 'A4' 'Pacific' No **60007** *Sir Nigel Gresley* climbs the gradient approaching Potters Bar on Sunday 28 September 1952, hauling the 09.15 King's Cross–York 'Centenarian Express' special which was run to commemorate, among other things, the opening of the London terminus. (Below) At the same spot, on Sunday 23 July 1989, the 08.50 local service from King's Cross to Welwyn Garden City is formed of Class '317/2' No 317365 in the livery of the Network SouthEast Sector. *Both BM*

POTTERS BAR (2): Three views of Potters Bar cutting taken on 12 May 1951, 16 July 1955 and 17 November 1989: (Top) Prior to the widening, Class 'N2/2' 0-6-2T No 69490, steaming freely, hauls two sets of 'Quadart' articulated coaches on a stopping service for Hatfield, indicated by the route destination board fitted. (Centre) Gresley Class 'V2' 2-6-2 No 60849 rasps up the gradient with a northbound Anglo-Scottish fitted freight soon after the cutting was widened to four tracks, but prior to the new tunnel bores being completed to enable the four track section to extend further south. (Bottom) The latest technology for the ECML, with the southbound 'Yorkshire Pullman' consisting of all Mk 4 stock headed by Driving Van Trailer No 82203, with Class '91' No 91009 propelling at the rear. *All BM*

The North London line

PALACE GATES: (Above) On 10 April 1954, a train for North Woolwich waits to leave Palace Gates station hauled by Holden Class 'F5' 2-4-2T No 67209. This station, near Wood Green, was closed in January 1963 when the spur from South Tottenham was abandoned and North London line services were extended to Gospel Oak. Contained within Bounds Green traction depot yard, a very small section of the platform end, furthest from the camera in this view, still remains today, but the whole of the station buildings have been totally eradicated by the construction of a modern housing estate, the present-day view (below) having been taken from the same standpoint in February 1989. *BM/KB*

STRATFORD (LOW LEVEL): (Above) The 12.45 Palace Gates–North Woolwich train pauses at Stratford (Low Level) station on 8 August 1953 headed by Class 'F5' 2-4-2T No 67219 running bunker first. Apart from the construction of a couple of wooden sheds, the elimination of semaphore signalling and a brick wall erected on the down platform, the present-day scene from the same viewpoint on 11 December 1989 (below) appears little altered as Class '313' EMU No 313011 enters the station forming the 11.43 Richmond–North Woolwich North London line service. *BM/KB*

FORK JUNCTION, STRATFORD: On 16 February 1957, Thompson Class 'L1' 2-6-4T No 67701 passes Fork Junction box as it restarts a North Woolwich–Palace Gates train from Stratford (Low Level) station and runs beneath the Liverpool Street–Norwich main line above. (Below) On 5 August 1989, the 14.35 North Woolwich–Richmond service is formed of Class '416/3' 2EPB unit No 6318; there is no Fork Junction signal box to pass, however, or even a Fork Junction, the line which branched off to Temple Mills having been closed in June 1969 and subsequently taken up. Even the motive power has since been returned to Southern Region, being replaced by Class '313s'. *R.C. Riley/BM*

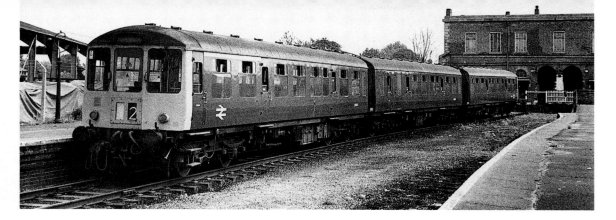

NORTH WOOLWICH: The arrival platform at North Woolwich station is now given over to the Great Eastern Museum where displays from the Passmore Edwards Museum Trust are housed both inside and outside the old station building. (Top) On 10 August 1973, however, that was the only platform in use, with the tracks on the departure side having been taken up. The three-car Birmingham R&CW Class '104' DMU forming the 12.54 train to Stratford (Low Level) was withdrawn in 1981-82. (Above) Sixteen years later to the day, the departure platform has been reinstated and is now the only one in use for British Rail services, a view of the Museum yard being possible over the fence which has been erected. The Class '416/3' EMU forming a service to Richmond is No 6308. *BM/KB*

(Left) The original 1847 Italianate North Woolwich station building was almost derelict when photographed on 6 April 1983 but, thanks to a sponsorship from the London Dockland Development Corporation, the building has since been completely restored. The view of what is now the Great Eastern Museum frontage was taken on 10 August 1989. *BM/KB*

173

The Poplar Docks line

DEVONS ROAD, BOW: Once boasting a North London Railway train every 15 minutes from Broad Street, bomb damage sustained by London's Docklands during the Second World War, coupled with a general decline in revenue, resulted in cessation of passenger services to Poplar from 14 May 1944. Tracks east of Millwall were taken up in 1967 and a direct line constructed from the NLR yard at Poplar to the western Poplar Docks across the bed of the erstwhile Blackwall Railway. This line replaced the old high-level ex-NLR access and remained in occasional use until the advent of the Docklands Light Railway. (Above) In connection with the then-projected Docklands Light Railway, a Cravens two-car DMU, consisting of motor brake and driving trailer cars Nos E53362/54420, was used on the line on 9 February 1984 to ascertain whether a regular and frequent train service would be likely to have any adverse noise or vibration effect upon the local buildings or their inhabitants in the event of an intensive train service coming about. The test train operated on the line for some five hours and is seen above near Devons Road, Bow. The present-day scene from the same viewpoint (right) shows a DLR driverless train approaching the Docklands station of Devons Road with the tell-tale high-rise flats still showing up in the background, although now partly obscured by the new building under construction on the left. *BM/KB*

174

DEVONS ROAD SHED: With some of the flats shown opposite under construction, the view (above) of Devons Road engine shed yard on 16 April 1955 shows an Ivatt Class '4MT' 'Mogul' No 43001 as originally constructed with a double chimney. Opened by the North London Railway in 1882, Devons Road (1D) closed for steam traction in 1958 and became the first all-diesel shed in Great Britain; final shutdown came about in 1964. Apart from the background flats, the site when the more recent view was taken in February 1989 was derelict. *BM/KB*

The 'Ally Pally'

ALEXANDRA PALACE: The Great Northern Railway branch from Highgate to Alexandra Palace, known as the 'Ally Pally' line, opened with the Palace itself on 24 May 1873 and initially brought great crowds. However, the fluctuating fortunes of the Palace following its destruction by fire on 9 June 1873 brought about no fewer than eight closures and re-openings of the line between 1873 and 1898, and it eventually closed for the last time on 5 July 1954. (Above) On 10 April 1954, the 14.45 auto-train for Finsbury Park leaves the terminus propelled by Hill Class 'N7/2' 0-6-2T No 69694. Behind the trees to the right of the present-day view can just be seen the Palace mast. *BM/KB*

CROUCH END: (Above) With the Class 'N7/2' No 69694 now leading the push-pull set and seemingly exuding steam from every crack in the bodysides, the 16.02 Finsbury Park–Alexandra Palace train restarts from the Crouch End stop on the same day. As can be observed from the present view of this location, photographed in February 1989, the old trackbed is now a footpath. *BM/KB*

The Southern's Thames-side termini

CHARING CROSS: For many years, nothing very much occurred to alter the appearance of Charing Cross station from its Southern Railway days, even the 'SR' initials and coat of arms being retained under Nationalisation. In the late 1980s, however, the value of the air space above the station platforms was realised by the BR Property Board, the result being the massive development which is shown (below) nearing completion on 17 December 1990 — and happily retaining a revised form of the original 'SR' insignia. The trains shown are the 13.23 to Hayes and the 13.33 to Dartford via Bexleyheath, both formed of Class '415/4' 4EPBs, Nos 5453 and 5454 respectively, which are the same type of units which filled all six platforms in the photograph dated 3 January 1959, albeit having been refurbished since and given a different livery. Following completion of Hungerford Bridge, the original Charing Cross station was opened by the South Eastern Railway in 1864 and, because of its location near Trafalgar Square, was considered as the most illustrious in London. Its fortunes have since risen and fallen with those of the Strand, at the western end of which the station stands. *R.C. Riley/BM*

CANNON STREET (1): (Above) On 25 April 1951, some eight years prior to the removal of the overall station roof, the fireman of Maunsell Class 'N15' 'King Arthur' 4-6-0 No 30806 *Sir Galleron* (the last of the 'Arthurs' to be built) has checked the coupling ready for an evening departure to Hastings. (Below) Seen from the same position on 7 June 1976, empty EPB stock awaits the 'crush hour' of 17.00 and the daily onslaught of City commuters. *Both BM*

CANNON STREET (2): The book jacket photographs show the situation just outside Cannon Street as it was in 1958 and with the new office development above the platforms in 1992; the two views on this page date from 1957 and 1976 and show, respectively, the inaugural non-steam service to Hastings on 6 May 1957 formed of diesel-electric multiple units Nos 1003 and 1004, and, below, the 15.01 to Hayes (Kent) departing on 7 June 1976 formed of Class '415' 4EPB stock Nos 5232 and 5234. *Both BM*

HOLBORN VIADUCT (1): Holborn Viaduct station opened in March 1874, followed by Snow Hill (later Holborn Viaduct Low Level) in August of the same year. Both provided much-needed relief to commuters who previously had been required to use the congested island platforms at Ludgate Hill station (closed in 1929), situated on the through line to Farringdon. Although closed in 1916, the Low Level platforms remained visible just inside Snow Hill tunnel, which was kept open until 1969 for through freight traffic, thereafter being out of use until the link to Farringdon was restablished for the introduction of 'Thameslink' services in April 1988. In order to gain access to the tunnel, the 'Thameslink' trains had to bypass the high-level Holborn Viaduct platforms, and that station ultimately closed in 1990. It was replaced by St Pauls Thameslink (later renamed City Thameslink), located near the site of the old Low Level platforms. On 18 August 1989 (above), the 15.38 Sevenoaks-Bedford 'Thameslink' train, formed of Class '319' EMU No 319019, enters Snow Hill tunnel, while trains to Dartford via Sidcup and to Canterbury East await departure time in Holborn Viaduct station alongside.

(Below) A massive engineering project has obliterated the high-level platforms, allowing the tracks into Snow Hill tunnel to be slewed to the right to gain access to Blackfriars station via a remarkable 1 in 29 gradient. On 29 May 1990, the same Class '319' unit forms the 08.50 Luton-Sevenoaks train, approaching the City Thameslink stop. Then the offices of Williams National House could still be seen above the remains of the Holborn Viaduct concourse, but today this scene is now underground, beneath new office complexes that have been constructed over the railway. *Both BM*

BLACKFRIARS: Originally named Blackfriars Bridge, the first station opened in 1864 on the east side of the approach to the new road bridge over the Thames then being constructed. The terminus then moved over the river to another short-lived site in Little Earl Street. Thereafter, the opening in 1865 of Ludgate Hill station catered for passengers until St Pauls station opened on the present-day site in 1886; its name was changed to Blackfriars when St Pauls Underground station was opened in 1937. (Above) On a very murky 10 October 1954 a Class 'T9' 'Greyhound' 4-4-0 No 30729 is the subject of attention from enthusiasts as it waits to leave one of the three terminus platforms with what is described on the headboard as an 'Inter-Regional Ramblers Special'.

(Below) Completely rebuilt between 1972 and 1977, the present-day Blackfriars is probably busier than at any time in its long history, with through all-day 'Thameslink' services from Bedford, Luton and St Albans to Brighton,

Sevenoaks and Guildford, and peak-time trains from the terminus platforms to Orpington and to Dartford via Sidcup. On a sunny 9 November 1991, Class '319' No 319029 restarts the 12.00 Luton-Guildford 'Thameslink' train from the southbound through platform, while in the three terminus platforms are Class '33/1' No 33114, with a charter to Sevenoaks, and two stabled 4EPB units. *R. C. Riley/BM*

182

LONDON BRIDGE (1): Two views of trains departing from the Central Section terminus of London Bridge graphically illustrate something of what has occurred to London's city skyline in the intervening 30 years; just one building, on the right, remains to show that the locations are the same. (Above) On 14 May 1959, Wainwright Class 'D1' 4-4-0 No 31735 draws away from the station with the 12.44 vans train for Ramsgate. (Below) On 18 August 1989, the 10.19 Sanderstead–London Bridge train enters the station formed of Class '423/1' 4VEP EMU No 3465; 4EPB and 4CIG stock is stabled awaiting the evening commuters and another 4EPB enters the Eastern Section of the station with a local service to Charing Cross. *R. C. Riley/BM*

LONDON BRIDGE (2): The half-barrel-shaped cast iron roof of the London, Brighton & South Coast Railway terminus of London Bridge has survived despite the ravages of time and, in particular, Adolf Hitler's bombs. (Above) On 14 May 1959, Billinton Class 'E4' 0-6-2T No 32474 steams away from beneath the roof hauling a short vans train bound for New Cross Gate. (Below) As can be observed from the similar view taken on 13 September 1982, the platforms have been lengthened and the whole station is now in the shadow of the multi-storey Guy's Hospital building to the rear. *R. C. Riley/BM*

LONDON BRIDGE (3): A modern colour-light signal gantry has replaced the old one and the water tower is but a memory of steam days. The modern London Bridge power box has been constructed in front of the station's terminus wall, but the multiplicity of trackwork remains, as do the 4EPB electric multiple units! (Above) On a dull 23 June 1951, a Marsh Class 'I3' 4-4-2T No 32091 is watered up as a 4EPB passes in the background from the Eastern Section lines. *Both BM*

LONDON BRIDGE (4): The station refurbishment completed at London Bridge in the 1980s was no more than the old buildings deserved, having only been patched up in one manner or another during the years following extensive damage sustained during the London Blitz. As London's first railway terminus, it was opened in 1836 as a simple two-platform structure for the London & Greenwich Railway which ran to Greenwich across brick arches. The view of Ivatt Class '2MT' 2-6-2T No 41300 running through Platform 2 on 13 March 1957 (above) contrasts with the new-look premises of 18 August 1989 (below), where can be seen the new platform canopies and passenger overbridge, if not the fresh paint. At Platform 2 is Class '415/1' 4EPB (what else?) No 5126 awaiting custom as the 11.19 shuttle to Cannon Street. *R. C. Riley/BM*

South London scenes

NORTH KENT WEST JUNCTION: (Above) Passing the signal box at North Kent West Junction on 29 March 1958, Maunsell Class 'W' 2-6-4T No 31919 heads a transfer freight to Hither Green. Until Bricklayers Arms shed was closed in 1962, all movements in and out had to made by way of this busy junction which, on 24 April 1989, still carried track slowly being hidden by the spreading undergrowth (below). Also still remaining in situ on the site was the base of the old signal gantry on the left. *R. C. Riley/KB*

DEPTFORD WHARF: A branch from Old Kent Road Junction, near New Cross Gate, opened on 2 July 1849, weaved a path beneath the London, Brighton & South Coast Railway main line and over the East London Line and made two crossings of the Grand Surrey Canal before reaching the River Thames at Deptford Wharf and Surrey Commercial Docks. Operated under the auspices of the LB&SCR and later the Southern Railway, the line lasted well into the days of British Rail and did not close finally until 1 January 1964. Today, however, it is but a memory; the Deptford Wharf swingbridge taking goods trains over the canal is now transformed into a footbridge taking pedestrians over the A206 road to the neighbouring industrial estate! On 29 March 1959, Billinton Class 'E6' 0-6-2T No 32417 crosses the Grand Surrey Canal with a freight. Almost exactly 30 years later, the scene has changed beyond all recognition. *R.C. Riley/Ken Brunt*

BRICKLAYERS ARMS SHED: The terminal station of Bricklayers Arms was jointly opened by the South Eastern Railway and the London & Croydon Railway in 1844 as a means of avoiding the tolls imposed by the London & Greenwich Railway for the use of its metals at London Bridge. The description of the station as a new 'Grand West End Terminus' would, today, have brought proceedings under the Trades Descriptions Act! The hoped-for passenger traffic did not materialise in sufficient volume for the venture to continue, and the two-road structure closed in 1852 and became the original Bricklayers Arms engine shed. The depot became the heart of the Bricklayers Arms goods complex and maintained locomotives used for passenger traffic from Charing Cross and Cannon Street to the Kent coast as well as myriad goods engines. The above view, taken on 2 April 1955, shows Class 'L1' 4-4-0 No 31788 alongside Class 'E4' 0-6-2T No 32564 outside the four-road extension to the complex which dated from 1865, albeit re-roofed by the Southern Railway since that time. 73B was closed in 1962 and a parcels depot was opened there in 1969, the site eventually being abandoned in 1981. (Below) Purchased from BR for much-needed housing development in the area, this was the view of the site on 29 July 1989 taken from the same standpoint. *Both BM*

NEW CROSS GATE: One platform of the ex-London, Brighton & South Coast Railway station at New Cross Gate (originally New Cross) is given over to the East London Line of London Underground where services run to and from Whitechapel. (Above) On 3 June 1956, the platform was used for a special ramblers' train, the 'John Milton Special', which travelled from there to Chesham with a London Transport locomotive on each end, there being no run-round facilities at the Buckinghamshire terminus for the return journey. With No 14 *Benjamin Disraeli* waiting to leave, there would seem to be little that has changed here over the years apart from a reduction in the length of the platform canopy and the hut having been painted white! (Below) On 28 December 1988, refurbished LT A60 stock, with Driving Motor Car No 5066 leading, waits to depart with the Whitechapel shuttle. *Both BM*

NEW CROSS GATE SHED (1): The complicated history of the rambling buildings that made up New Cross (later New Cross Gate) engine shed began in June 1839 when the London & Croydon Railway opened a roundhouse there. Under the auspices of the LB&SCR and later the Southern Railway, the depot was extended on a number of occasions and for many years was important as the Brighton line's main London depot. Electrification and the transfer of maintenance to other depots resulted in closure in 1957, although no locomotives were allocated there after 1949 due to the buildings being open to the elements as a result of bomb damage sustained during the war. 'New shed' was constructed in 1929, although it looked anything but new on 23 June 1951 (above) with Billinton Class 'E3' 0-6-2T No 32459 simmering outside. Apart from one outside wall, nothing is left standing of the old complex today, the view below being taken from the same position on 28 December 1989. *BM/KB*

NEW CROSS GATE SHED (2): (Above) Where Bulleid's unsteamed second 'Leader' Class 0-6-6-0T No 39002 was dumped on 23 June 1951, an oil storage tank stands today. On the day following the photograph being taken, the locomotive was towed to Brighton Works and cut up. *Both BM*

HITHER GREEN SHED: Primarily concerned with freight locomotives, Hither Green shed was opened by the Southern Railway in 1933 and closed to steam in 1961. Thereafter converted for diesel traction, it was downgraded to a locomotive stabling and fuelling point in 1985 but is currently seeing a new lease of life as the depot mainly involved with the extensive freight traffic for Channel Tunnel construction. (Above) On 2 May 1959, new Class '24' diesel-electric locomotives are lined up at 73C alongside the steam engines which they were intended to replace, and which include a variety of Maunsell 'Moguls', Wainwright 'C' Class 0-6-0s and a Bulleid Class 'Q1' 0-6-0. (Below) From atop the same lighting mast, the photograph taken on 29 July 1989 shows the completion of the two-lane fuelling shed (which in 1959 had only received its concrete base) and Class '33' and '73' locomotives awaiting their next duty. *R. C. Riley/BM*

DENMARK HILL (1): On 14 May 1959, Maunsell three-cylinder Class 'N1' 'Mogul' No 31876 scurries through Denmark Hill station with an excursion from Victoria to Ramsgate and contrasts with the scene below, taken on 9 August 1982, of Class '415/1' 4EPB No 5220 in the station and forming the 16.50 Holborn Viaduct–Bellingham local stopping train. King's College Hospital and its laundry chimney now dominate the background, only some rubble marks the position of the signal box, and the station building has suffered fire damage, the top portion having been destroyed. This was later to be rebuilt, however, and today bears more resemblance to the steam age view than the one from 1982. *R. C. Riley/BM*

DENMARK HILL (2): Stabling facilities for locomotive-hauled carriage stock in the 1950s were not over-plentiful, and often rather out-of-the-way sidings had to be utilised during the daytime to await morning or evening peak services. (Above) The 15.40 empty coaching stock working from Blackheath yards in South East London, to form the 18.14 Cannon Street–Ramsgate, is taken through Denmark Hill station on 6 May 1959 by Wainwright 'C' Class 0-6-0 No 31717; the uncommon disc code signifies a North Kent Lines train via Nunhead. When the comparison photograph was taken on 25 November 1989, embankment foliage precluded exactly the same footsteps being used to record the 10.51 Sevenoaks–Cricklewood service, formed of Class '319' EMU No 319007, but little appears to have changed apart from demolition of the building on the embankment which was once a sub-station for the LB&SCR overhead electrified lines. *R. C. Riley/BM*

PECKHAM RYE (1): (Above) Passing Peckham Rye coal sidings, north of the station, on 10 October 1953, two old-type 4SUB EMUs, led by No 4207, form a London Bridge to London Bridge local circular service travelling via Forest Hill, Crystal Palace and Tulse Hill. (Below) On 29 July 1989, the 11.12 train from West Sutton to London Bridge is formed of Class '455/8' EMU No 5802 and passes the same point; the coal sidings have long since disappeared and the track on which the train is travelling has been slewed. The old warehouse on the left of the scene, which rather looked as if it was likely to fall down at any minute, in fact still survives to the present day. Looks are not everything! *R. C. Riley/KB*

PECKHAM RYE (2): (Above) On 28 February 1957, Class 'W' 2-6-4T No 31923 hauls a freight for Hither Green past the Peckham Rye depot built in 1908-9 by the LB&SCR for maintenance and repair of its South London line overhead electric stock. (Below) On 29 July 1989, the 10.42 Cricklewood–Sevenoaks 'Thameslink' service, formed of Class '319' No 319048, passes the same spot. An unusual-looking gathering of new dwellings now occupies the depot site, and on the opposite side of the line the old houses have gone, converted into the Warwick Gardens parkland, a site proposed for the emergence into daylight of the underground high-speed rail link for the Channel Tunnel! *R. C. Riley/BM*

Kent suburbs

BECKENHAM HILL: The Catford Loop line from Nunhead to Shortlands was opened in 1892 and became an accepted relief route for the LC&DR main line via Penge East, served today by local trains from Blackfriars to Sevenoaks and also by 'Thameslink' services. With Catford being the 1910 limit of the London built-up area, and the Ravensbourne valley above Catford remaining unbuilt over, the station constructed on the line at Beckenham Hill was reputed to be the quietest of suburban stations until the edge of the London County Council's Bellingham estate reached it. (Above) A Ramsgate train heads through Beckenham Hill on 9 May 1959 in the charge of Maunsell 'Schools' Class 4-4-0 No 30938 *St Olave's.* (Below) The same view today is a little obscured as Class '319' No 319046 draws to a halt, forming the 12.11 Cricklewood–Sevenoaks train. The attractive old wooden footbridge on the station has been replaced by a metal one and a block of flats has appeared on the horizon above the houses, but everything else appears to have remained substantially the same. *R. C. Riley/BM*

SHORTLANDS JUNCTION: Rounding the curve between Shortlands and Beckenham Junction at Shortlands Junction, 'Schools' Class 4-4-0 No 30916 *Whitgift* (above) heads for London Victoria with a train from Ramsgate on 27 July 1957, photographed by Dick Riley from the bottom of his garden. Today's aspect is somewhat different, having been widened for four tracks and featuring a signal box, built for the widening, which has since been closed following introduction of the London Bridge power box. Semaphore signalling has disappeared but the sub-station still operates, although it is becoming more and more obscured by foliage in the same manner as the grass bank which made an identical position for a present-day photograph impossible. On 30 November 1989, a Class '411/4' 'Kent Coast' EMU, No 1505, in NSE livery, forms the 12.15 Ramsgate–Victoria service. *R. C. Riley/KB*

BICKLEY JUNCTION (1): (Above) Topping the 1 in 95/100 climb from Shortlands Junction to Bickley Junction on 27 July 1955, Maunsell Class 'N15' 'King Arthur' 4-6-0 No 30769 *Sir Balan* makes little of a ten-coach Ramsgate train travelling on what is today the London-bound track at this point. Long winter shadows were evident on 12 November 1989 (below) as the 10.23 Victoria–Dover Western Docks service passes, formed of Class '411/5' 4CEP stock and led by No 1530 in 'Jaffa cake' livery. Despite the signal gantry and telegraph poles having disappeared and houses having been built, the general appearance of this particular stretch of the ex-South Eastern & Chatham Railway main line seems relatively unchanged. *BM/KB*

BICKLEY JUNCTION (2): (Above) On 8 November 1952 the 10.00 'Continetal Express' from Victoria to Dover, carrying passengers for Brussels, comes off the main line at Bickley and rounds the down loop to Petts Wood Junction, which connects the Victoria main line with that from Charing Cross. In connection with the first phase of the Kent Coast electrification of the late 1950s and early 1960s, the loop was re-designed and re-aligned in order to raise the line speed, and the junction at this point was moved back nearly 100 yards to where the 11.32 Victoria-Orpington train, consisting of Class '415/4' EPB No 5452, was photographed on 12 November 1989; the bridge supports to the right of the first coach in the 1952 view are still in position to the right of the modern view, with the bridge having been extended at this point to allow for the widening to four tracks. To allow for increased capacity following the opening of the Channel Tunnel, the old loop alignment has since been uncovered once again and four tracks now diverge at this point. *BM/KB*

ST MARY CRAY–CHISLEHURST LOOP: With a haul of Kent coal, Maunsell Class 'N' 'Mogul' No 31404 traverses the loop which connects the up main line to Victoria with that from Charing Cross. Since the above photograph was taken, on 21 February 1953, the rather mushy grassland bounding the line has become completely overgrown and a very large bramble thicket today prevents coverage from exactly the same spot. (Below) On 12 November 1989, a Class '930' 'Sandite and De-icing' train, No 008, is seen at the same position, formed from a redundant Class '405/2' 4SUB unit. *Both BM*

CHISLEHURST (1): (Above) With Chislehurst station in the background obscured by the exhaust of 'Schools' Class 4-4-0 No 30905 *Tonbridge,* this view of a down Hastings express, taken on 21 April 1951, is identical to the one of Class '202' 6L Hastings units Nos 1011 and 1031 (below) forming the 17.23 Charing Cross–Hastings train over 24 years later, on 19 May 1975. There is no exhaust now to obscure the station buildings, but the branch of a tree which has grown up has achieved the same result! *Both BM*

BOW WORKS: The North London Railway works at Bow were fully established as early as 1863 and once covered an area of 31 acres on both sides of the NLR main line. Overhaul of steam locomotives carried on well into the 1950s and work on carriages and wagons did not cease until the mid-1960s. The site was demolished by 1970 and today is solely residential, as indicated by the scene below, taken from almost exactly the same position as the one above, which shows the interior of the works on 16 April 1955 with three types of engine under repair: in the foreground is ex-LT&SR Class '3P' 'Atlantic' tank No 41941 with Class '3F' 'Jinty' 0-6-0T No 47487 behind and Stanier Class '4MT' 2-6-4T No 42514 in the adjoining bay. *BM/KB*

BARKING: (Above) On 23 March 1957, to the east of Barking station, Fairburn Class '4MT' 2-6-4T No 42520 hauls a LT&S lines train from the Essex coast towards Fenchurch Street while, on 1 December 1989, the 12.42 Fenchurch Street–Shoeburyness train is formed of Network SouthEast Sector-liveried Class '302' EMU No 302217. The houses to the right of the line remain, but an additional track has been installed and the yards on the left are now used exclusively by London Underground District Line trains. To the left of the present-day scene, an underpass for London-bound trains has been constructed by London Transport, displacing a number of lines. Semaphore signalling has, of course, disappeared, and ugly overhead electrification masts abound. *R. C. Riley/BM*

PURFLEET: Purfleet was one of the original stations opened by the LT&SR from Forest Gate to Tilbury in 1854. (Above) An afternoon Fenchurch Street–Shoeburyness train draws to a halt on 23 March 1957 powered by BR Standard '4MT' 2-6-4T No 80105. In contrast (below), on 7 July 1989, a similar service is formed of a Class '308' EMU No 308151. The station footbridge and up-side platform buildings have gone and undisturbed foliage appears to be taking over the area above the down side, where the track itself could do with a visit from the 'weed-killer' train. *R. C. Riley/KB*

GRAYS: (Above) On 23 March 1957, Ivatt Class '4MT' 'Mogul' No 43120 of Cricklewood shed approaches Grays station with a boat train for Tilbury Riverside. Chalk outcrops along the north bank of the River Thames brought about the establishment of a lime and cement industry in the area and emissions of the type seen top left were commonplace. Health and Safety regulations resulted in closure, however, and the same chimneys seen behind the undergrowth in the present-day photograph (below) are destined for demolition. The houses alongside the line appear to have lost a number of their chimneys but, otherwise, little change is apparent today apart from the siding with the buffer-stop becoming a through line. Forming the 10.42 service from Upminster to Tilbury Riverside on 1 December 1989 is Class '302' EMU No 302272. *R. C. Riley/KB*

Essex byways

OCKENDON: The 6 miles 53 chains connecting single line from Upminster to West Thurrock Junction, Grays, was opened by the LT&SR on 1 July 1892 and has just one intermediate station and passing loop at Ockendon. (Above) Approaching that station on 19 July 1952, a typical Grays–Upminster train of the immediate post-war period is hauled by Whitelegg ex-LT&SR '2F' 0-6-2T No 41986, whose name, *Canvey Island,* was short-lived, being removed circa 1912. (Below) A present-day branch train at the same location on 5 August 1989, the 16.08 Upminster–Grays, is formed of Class '302' EMU No 302223. *BM/KB*

EPPING: The Central Line of London Underground reached Epping in 1949, the extension having been abandoned pre-war, but the Epping–Ongar services remained steam-hauled until 1957. (Above) On 8 August 1953, the 11.32 Epping–Ongar train awaits departure behind ex-Great Eastern Railway Class 'F5' 2-4-2T No 67213 of Stratford shed, which has just finished watering up. (Below) On 9 September 1988, 1962 London Underground stock forms the 07.50 service to Ongar; the water column is long gone, the platform has been resurfaced and the chimneys on the station house have received attention. Otherwise, the general flavour of a Great Eastern country station remains at this present-day London Transport outpost. *BM/KB*

EPPING SHED: Epping was one of ten sub-sheds attached to Stratford depot (30A). Seen on 8 August 1953, this building dates from 1949, the original 1893 two-road edifice having, almost literally, fallen down of its own volition. Following the arrival of London Underground, remaining steam workings, freights, excursions and the Ongar push-pull trains were operated from here until electrification was completed to Ongar in November 1957 when the little shed finally closed. (Above) On shed on 8 August can be seen two ex-Great Eastern 'J15' Class 0-6-0s, Nos 65444 and 65449, and a push-pull-fitted ex-Great Northern 'C12' Class 'Atlantic' tank No 67363; the two tender engines were used for light freight workings to Temple Mills and Ongar, and the tank engine was tried out on the push-pull trains to and from Ongar but was not particularly successful and stayed only for the one summer. (Below) Nothing now remains of the depot site, the area having become the station car park. *BM/KB*

EMERSON PARK: The 3¹/₂-mile branch line which connects Romford with Upminster was opened in 1893 as part of an LT&SR route to Tilbury via Upminster and Grays; the one intermediate station at Emerson Park opened in 1909 as a result of housing development in the area. (Above) On 19 July 1952, the 14.43 train from Romford to Upminster calls at the station hauled by an ex-Midland Railway '1P' Class 0-4-4T No 58054. With platform extended, changes to the small station building apparent, and a raised bridge constructed to allow for overhead electrification, the 13.53 service from Romford to Upminster (below) runs into the station on 23 February 1989 formed by Class '315' EMU No 315801. *BM/KB*

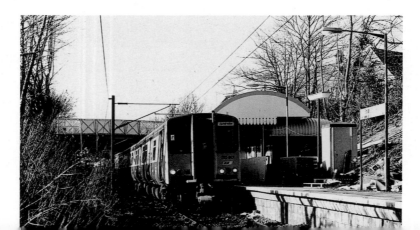

ROMFORD: The present-day Romford station dates from an LNER reconstruction of 1931. The original building was the terminus of the Eastern Counties Railway for one year from 1839 until the line was extended through to Brentwood in 1840. The LT&SR branch to Upminster was opened on 7 June 1893 and was conceived mainly to keep the then rival Great Eastern Railway away from Tilbury, even having its own station entrance until 1934. (Above) Ex-Midland Railway Johnson '1P' Class 0-4-4T No 58038 propels the 12.14 train from Upminster into Romford station on 5 September 1953. Class '315' EMUs now operate the service and the photograph below of No 315801, taken from the same spot, was not made any easier by the forces of nature endeavouring to reclaim the line for their own. *BM/KB*

LIVERPOOL STREET (1): Considered by many to have been the most picturesque of the London termini, Liverpool Street station dates from 1874 and was designed by the Great Eastern Railway engineer Edward Wilson. There were a number of alterations to the station in the course of its long and busy history, but nothing in any way matching up to the redevelopment that commenced in 1983, and was eventually completed in December 1991, when a quite magnificent new station was opened by HM the Queen. The Western Train Shed and Great Eastern Hotel have both been retained, and the remainder of the refurbishment has been totally sympathetic to the original structure, with the old pattern of long and short platforms now replaced by ones of uniform length, with eight tracks out to Bethnal Green. The overall scheme was part of the massive Broadgate development which involved the closure and complete obliteration of Broad Street station (see page 262). The sulphorous interior of the Liverpool Street steam-hauled suburban lines is graphically illustrated above by ex-GER 'N7/2' Class 0-6-2T No 69681 simmering under a May sun in 1951, waiting to depart with a train for Hertford East. The present-day view (below) from the same position shows part of the massive concrete raft erected above the suburban platforms, from which Class '305' EMU No 305415 wiats to emerge, forming a service for Bishops Stortford. *Both BM*

LIVERPOOL STREET (2): On 10 September 1977, a view looking towards the station through the washing plant reveals Class '37' No 37025 and Class '47/0' No 47005 at the stabling point awaiting their next duty. (Below) The view from the same position in June 1991 shows Class '312/0' EMU No 312702 leaving the station from beneath part of the Broadgate development, forming the 15.10 service for Braintree. *Both BM*

LIVERPOOL STREET (3): The above view of the Liverpool Street main-line departure platforms on 11 April 1951 shows Class 'B1' 4-6-0 No 61250 awaiting departure time with a Norwich express, and No 61264 of the same class backing out of the station following release from the buffer-stops. (Below) From the same position, on 18 August 1989, the camera is beneath the new concrete raft where, in the distance, a four-car Class '312' EMU No 312791 makes up the 13.42 train to Harwich Town. *Both BM*

BETHNAL GREEN BANK: After leaving Liverpool Street station, the lines take almost a 45 degree turn to the right before commencing the climb of Bethnal Green bank at 1 in 70. (Above) The 17.54 Liverpool Street–Norwich express approaches Bethnal Green station on 1 June 1958 hauled by BR Standard 'Britannia' 'Pacific' No 70007 *Coeur de Lion* and passes a Class 'N7' 0-6-2T labouring up the incline with a stopping train for Enfield Town. (Below) From the same position on 5 August 1989, Class '309/3' EMU No 309613 heads for Clacton, passing over white newly-laid ballast. A few of the background buildings remain on the right, but the left-hand side of the scene is completely changed, with tall city offices now on the horizon and the old sidings taken up. *BM/KB*